book by

Charles F. Haanel

author of *The Master Key System*

A
BOOK
ABOUT
YOU

Edited by Anthony R. Michalski

KALLISTI PUBLISHING
WILKES-BARRE, PA

W9-BOH-363

Other books by Charles F. Haanel...

The Master Key System
The Master Key Workbook
Master Key Arcana
The Amazing Secrets of the Yogi
Mental Chemistry
The New Psychology

Other books published by Kallisti Publishing...

Size Matters!
Getting Connected Through Exceptional Leadership
Road Map for National Security: Imperative for Change
Walk, Don't Run

Kallisti Publishing
332 Center Street, Wilkes-Barre, PA 18702
Phone (877) 444-6188 • Fax (419) 781-1907
www.kallistipublishing.com

Kallisti Publishing titles may be purchased for business or promotional use or for special sales. Please contact Kallisti Publishing for more information.

Kallisti Publishing and its logo are trademarks of Kallisti Publishing.

First Edition
10 9 8 7 6 5 4 3 2 1

Library of Congress Control Number: 2005930641
ISBN 0-9761111-2-8

DESIGNED AND PRINTED IN THE UNITED STATES OF AMERICA

WWW.KALLISTIPUBLISHING.COM

"This above all: To thine own self be true,
And it must follow, as the night the day,
Thou canst not then be false to any man."

A Book About You

Table of Contents

Foreword

Introduction.. 1
Planetary Vibrations............................ 7
Solar Vibrations....................................... 17
Mental Vibrations 25
Electrical Vibrations 35
Celestial Vibrations............................49
Cosmic Vibrations................................. 65
Light Vibrations 75
Sound Vibrations 85
Color Vibrations 91
Heat Vibrations 99
Periodicity 109
The Source of Life...............................123
The Emotions 135
Magnetism..143
The Imagination 155
Destiny... 163

Index
Biography of Charles F. Haanel

WWW.BOOKABOUTYOU.COM

Foreword

This book is about you. I cannot think of a book that details and describes one's place in the cosmic setting and how the cosmic setting can and does influences a person like this book does. Although many books have been written about the subjects that Mr. Haanel tackles in this book, I can think of none that match this book. Much like how *The Master Key System* by Haanel is a definitive success and attainment philosophy, this book is a definitive statement about you and the things that make you.

As you read this book, you will learn about a plethora of subjects: astronomy, astrology, physics, alchemy, and many more. It is not to be taken lightly. Some may say that astrology is something that should be relegated to the entertainment section of less reputable newspapers. I say to give this a shot!

Astrology has a long history. It was the original study of the stars and the cosmos. Unfortunately, is was bastardized and compromised by many hundreds—if not thousands—of false prophets and charlatans.

In this volume you are holding, Mr. Haanel attempts to set the record straight, so to speak. He approaches the subject in a sober and logical way. He does not say that if one is a Gemini, then he will be this or that because the stars guide him; rather, he says that "The stars incline, but they do not compel!" In other words, while the influences may be there, they do not predict nor do they impel one to act one way or another.

Haanel's idea is basically this: That we as human beings in a large and unknown universe can be and are influenced by the various forces that interact upon us from the various bodies that inhabit our solar system and galaxy, but ultimately, we all enjoy free will.

This might be difficult for some to swallow, but there is very real and tangible proof that celestial bodies do in fact influence us. For example, does not the Moon influence the tides of the oceans? or the menstrual cycle of women? or the mental state of people? That should be proof enough that we can be influenced by the vibrations of celestial bodies. The only thing that is up for examination is how far does the influence extend?

The idea that we are swimming in a sea of vibrations from each other, from the Earth, and from celestial bodies is a proven fact. The notion that all physical objects—matter—is made up of an almost uncountable numbers of electrons is a proven fact. The perception that science is continually discovering evidence that what many thought was humbug is actually possible or even true is a proven fact.

This is what *A Book About You* attempts to convey to you: that you are a conscious mind that is influenced by the many different vibrations that travel in our universe. Nothing more; nothing less.

In this book, you will learn quite a few things about yourself.

- You'll see how everything in the universe is vibrating and how the vibrations reach out to you.

- You'll discover what your astrological sign really means and why the traits of that sign become tendencies in you.

- You will learn about the law of periodicity and how to use it to your advantage.

- You will gain a clearer view of your life and how you can take advantage of the myriad opportunities around you.

- You will understand the science behind astrology.

- You will learn how to deal with people on a greater level than you ever imagined because you will truly understand them.

- You will truly become aware of your free will, which is the ultimate gateway to freedom and prosperity.

In the tradition of *The Master Key System*, this book is not one that you will read once never to read again. Quite the contrary. This is one of those books that will become a reference for your many questions and inquiries. You will read this book as you find yourself asking questions about things you see and experience in the world.

If I may, though, give a few words of caution: Take it slowly and ask lots of questions.

As with most things in life, learning what is in this book is a race of endurance and not speed. Take the time to understand. If you doubt something, then research it until you prove it either right or wrong. When you study this book, you are studying yourself. Hopefully, when you are done reading, you will have a greater understanding of yourself and the world—and universe—around you.

Most of all and above everything, enjoy the learning and the process. If at first something does not make sense to you, then set it aside and return to it later. When you're ready for it, try to tackle it again.

This is truly a book about you. With the knowledge and understanding that you gain from this book, it is my hope that you endeavour to do great things and accomplish all of your goals.

Have fun...

Tony Michalski
Kallisti Publishing

A Book About You

WWW.KALLISTIPUBLISHING.COM

INTRODUCTION

Matter in motion and ether under strain constitute the fundamental principles with which we have to do in physics. These are both vibratory activities.

We speak of them as if there were two principles; there is, however, but one principle with a dual manifestation: it is cause and effect. Matter in motion puts ether[1] under strain, ether under strain puts matter into motion.

All phenomena in the Universe are the result of the operation of this basic principle. Let us check up on those with which we are most familiar.

POWER

Force, all power, energy—call it what you will—resolves itself into two divisions: kinetic and potential. Kinetic is actual power and is invariably associated with motion. There can be no motion without something to move. Kinetic power is, therefore, matter is motion. Potential power is power at rest, reserve power, power distributed through all space, or ether under strain.

All force, all power, all energy is then a vibratory activity.

LIGHT

The Earth is one of the major bodies of our solar system. As it pushes its way around the Sun with the speed of a cannon ball, it puts

---

[1] While the concept of the ether has gone out of fashion, some modern quantum physical theories point to something that is similar to the ether. String Theory and Super String Theory are examples of modern theories that may point to what the "ether" could be. Dr. Frank Meno of the University of Pittsburgh theorizes that space is indeed filled with a substance; he calls that substance the "aether."

the ether under strain, and in doing so causes the atmosphere which consists of atoms of hydrogen and nitrogen to become incandescent; we thus have the phenomena of light.

Light is then a vibratory activity.

Heat

But the Earth not only moves through space which is filled with ether with the speed of a cannon ball, but it rotates upon its axis at the rate of two thousand miles an hour at its greatest circumference[1], with a gradually decreasing rate of motion until we reach the poles, where there is little or no motion.

This revolution of the Earth constitutes matter in motion as a cause and ether under strain as an effect; but this time the result is heat, the greatest amount of heat being found at the equator where strain upon the ether is greatest, with continually diminishing amount of heat until we reach the poles where there is no motion and consequently no heat.

Heat, then, is a vibratory activity.

Sound

Sound is the sensation produced as a result of matter in motion, which results in ether under strain. A word spoken in any part of the world changes the relative positions of the atoms of which the atmosphere is composed. This change is registered in the ether, which is so inconceivably subtle and vibrant, that every tone, every letter, every syllable is transmitted to every part of the world, and possibly to any other world; for this reason a man may make an address or sing a song in New York and millions of persons may sit in their own homes and listen to every word.

---

[1] According to modern measurements, the rotational speeed of the Earth at the equator is roughly 1,038 miles per hour.

The sound is originally caused by matter in motion, but it is carried upon the wings of the ether, the most volatile and active substance of which we can have any conception.

Sound is then a vibratory activity.

COLOR

Color is the result of the vibratory activity of atoms of matter or matter in motion. As the frequency increases, the vibrations become shorter and more rapid, the color changes, each change in color being due to a change in the rate of vibration.

MIND

Consciousness is the inner and thought the outward expression of Mind. Every human being and most animals have innumerable aerials, all reaching out into space ready to contact every thought, every inspiration, every indication of danger that their immediate environment may contain. These minute aerials or hairs, one of which is attached to every pore of the body, are stirred into activity by the vibrations from the Sun. When the Sun sinks behind the horizon, they, like the Arabs, "Fold their tents and silently steal away."[1] We are then no longer conscious, we go to sleep. Consciousness then is a vibratory activity and is due to the vibrations which reach us from the Sun.

All space is the store room of energy, which emanates from the Sun, and consciousness is caused by the contact of the human brain with the electro-magnetic vibrations of which the luminiferous ether is composed and which have their source in the Sun. Each of the planets is passing through this electro-magnetic field of force, forming an electro-magnetic field of its own.

These vibrations are being constantly impressed upon the ether and are received by each individual in accordance with his ability to

---

[1] From the poem "The Day is Done" by Henry Wadsworth Longfellow.

receive, for the brain is a receiving instrument and must be in tune with the vibration, otherwise, it does not register.

Mind or consciousness is then a vibratory activity.

LIFE

The personal constituents of a mob might be exactly the same as those of an army, the difference is that one is organized and one is not. A single atom is not material, it is simply a definite amount of energy, and by itself would be absolutely immaterial, but when these atoms are combined and organized, they assume the characteristics of the whole, of which they are a part. A part cannot be equal to the whole. On the other hand, the whole cannot be greater than all of its parts collectively and organically. Each part is as essential to the whole as the whole is to the part.

If, then, an organism is conscious and intelligent, the atoms of which that organism is composed must be conscious and intelligent, just as a single soldier might have a very small amount of power, but if combined with a hundred thousand other similar soldiers and thoroughly drilled and organized, a very considerable amount of power would be developed.

The atom, of which all organic or inorganic substance is created, is immaterial, conscious, and intelligent. The degree of consciousness and intelligence that is manifested in an organic body will then depend upon whether the mob spirit or the spirit of efficiency and service prevails.

The individual atom has no density. Density is an attribute of matter, and one atom has no material attributes; it is only when millions of them are organized into form that they assume material attributes.

The atom is the unit and man is an organization of these units. As Mr. Edison says, "I believe that our bodies are made up of myriads of units of life, we have assumed that the unit is man, which we can see, and have ignored the existence of the real life units, which are those we cannot see."

The aggregate of these life units is the ether, which embodies the ultimate spiritual principle and represents the unity of the forces and energies from which spring all the phenomena known to man, whether physical, mental, or spiritual.

Such vibrations are, however, not the result of motion in one direction.

The planets, which are gigantic dynamos, not only push their way through the ether at an incredible speed, but they revolve upon their axis and thus twist the ether into spiral form, the lines of force which reach us from the various planets consist therefore of vibrations in spiral form.

When these lines of force are crossed by a second or a third planet, the electrons necessarily revolve around each other, and the first step in organization takes place. The electron[1] is then no longer a point mass, but a mass having an axis of rotation, an arc orbit. The rapidity of motion, the size and shape of electrons involved, determine the nature of the atom which is eventually evolved.

As long as the electrons continue to move indefinitely, they remain electrons. But when they are grouped in a definite system, revolving about a central nucleus like a miniature solar system, they then constitute an atom of matter.

These units, aggregated into different systems, form the elements. From the elements, in more complex combination, the chemical substances are made. The inorganic substances are relatively simple combinations of bases and acids. The organic substances are more complexly compounded, and these substances, or some of them when arranged in a mechanism called a cell, are capable of certain process-

---

[1] At the time this book was written, the electron was thought to be the smallest particle of nature. Of course, since then scientists have discovered many more and much smaller particles. This is not to say that Haanel was incorrect in saying that something was being influenced, only that his nomenclature represented the knowledge of the time.

es: assimilation, excretion, growth, sensation, reproduction.

When an organism works in a self-sustaining system, we say that it is alive.

Form

Form is the result of the concentration of matter, and the concentration of matter implies the dissipation of motion. Wherever there is an aggregation of matter, there must be an equal absorption of motion.

Involution and evolution alternate indefinitely. Both processes are going on every instant, the ebb and flow of the forces of nature are ceaseless.

All form, organic or inorganic, is the result of the combination of Earth, Air, Fire, and Water, and each of these in turn are derived directly or indirectly from the Sun. Without the energizing rays from the Sun, there could be no possible motion.

The Solar fluid is the Ether, which holds in the solution every possible form of matter. This ether in a state of high vibration is the breath of life, in its lower vibration it is inorganic form, or matter.

All form is then a vibratory activity.

Section One

Planetary Vibrations

At birth you received a certain vibration consisting of the combination of ethereal vibrations existing at the moment. This vibration was impressed upon you very much as a note from an orchestra may be transmitted by the stylus of a phonograph to the sensitive wax receiver[1] with every single note and every shade of tone intact.

Thus the time of birth determined the nature and intensity of the vibrations which are apparent in your mental, moral, spiritual, and physical characteristics, and these in turn indicate the character, environment and opportunities which will come to you.

This does not mean that you are to flounder in a morass of destructive fatalism. On the contrary, it is simply indicative of the opportunities which will be presented or the temptations which will come; there is no denial of the self-determination or free will. You may use the characteristics given to you at birth, or change them as you will.

The particular nature of the vibrations which you receive at birth are but the tools of the workman, and the one who becomes the "ruler of his stars" is the one who does not complain because he was given a violin rather than a harp, for each piece is necessary in the grand symphony of life.

But because there is that within you by which you may transcend environment and heredity, is this any reason for withholding from you the nature of the implements upon which you must depend? Would you rather have the most complete information possible concerning the tools with which you must carve out the destiny which is yours? Will the one who knows nothing of the dangers and pitfalls which lie

---

[1] Here, Haanel is speaking of the phonographs of his day which utilized a wax cylinder to hold the recording. These wax cylinders evolved into records and then into CDs and digital music.

before him have a better opportunity than the one who has a map with each of these dangers carefully charted?

It requires superior wisdom to be the custodian of wisdom, and your ability to *obtain* is conditioned upon your ability to *attain*. Fear[1] becomes the parent of superstition, the insurmountable barrier to realization.

When the Sun is in major aspect with any planet, the individual nature and quality of such planet is conjoined with the terrestrial magnetism, hence the Zodiac, the space in which the various planets move, holds in solution every element of which your body is composed.

The Sun is the distributor of all life; it therefore contains the essence of which all the planets are composed, each of which expresses one of the factors evolved from the cosmic system.

As the vibrations from the Sun reach the planets, each one appropriates and embodies one dominant ray, and while the particular ray which is differentiated by each planet is again sent out to all of the signs of the Zodiac, it is focused in the particular sign over which the planet rules.

Then each planet acts as a reflector for one of the seven dominant rays of the Sun. After their cycle of differentiation and accomplishment has been completed, they are again gathered up and united in the one great white light.

The Sun is the creative center, it contains the primal germ of mind, it is the unmanifest, during time inconceivable this unmanifest has been manifesting, and that which has become manifest is the planetary system of Divine Creation.

The Sun, therefore, contains within itself the essence of all the planets and they themselves are but the medium through which and

---

[1] In *The Master Key System*, Haanel refers to fear as "the one arch enemy of the Solar Plexus" and that it "must be absolutely destroyed before there is any possibility of letting any light shine." When put together, all of Haanel's books ultimately teach one how to eliminate fear and doubt from life.

by which the forces of the Sun are differentiated. Manifestation in the objective proceeds through the operation of the principles of construction and differentiation. Life is the process by which the ethereal substance, which scintillates from the center of the molecule, manifests on form.

The vibrations received from the Sun represent the principle of immortality. They are pure Being or life Itself.

The vibrations received from the Moon represent the mortal or all that comprise the personality, all that is mortal; thus the vibrations from the Sun and Moon manifest as Spirit and Matter, Soul and Body.

The vibrations from Mercury manifest as the intellect or mind; from Venus as love and emotion; from Mars as energy and force; from Jupiter as sympathy and devotion; from Saturn as perseverance and tenacity; from Uranus as renewal and change; from Neptune as religion and mysticism; and from the Earth as materialism and disintegration.

The ancients knew the Moon as Isis, the Queen of Heaven. It represents the mother of the female principle of life and is essentially feminine. It may be termed the giver of form.

The influence of the Moon upon tides, planting, and upon all unborn life has been known to the world for countless ages. Its peculiar influence upon women is well known, yet seldom connected with the fact. And physicians are beginning to realize that most diseases have certain cycles of periodicity which may be directly attributed to the Moon's motion. That fact was familiar to the wise men of all past ages.

Its rapid transit through the heavens brings to a focus the many aspects—good and bad—found in every person, dormant perhaps until an angle is formed which sets in motion vibrations beyond human control. Thus we have the sudden accidents, the flare of ungoverned temper, and likewise the never-to-be forgotten moments of ecstasy.

The rays of the Sun are differentiated through the spleen. The altered conditions of the Sun's rays become vitality; it is a force downward. In the same way the mind is an elemental essence which is pouring down into manifestation, and as it passes through our brain, we specialize or educate it, moulding it by our will into the thought-forms which constitute thought and lead finally to action.

Every body attracts every other body in proportion to its mass, and inversely in accordance with the distance. For this reason the Sun has a greater influence upon Mercury than upon Mars, more influence upon Venus than upon the Earth, more upon Mars than upon Jupiter, and more upon Saturn than upon Uranus.

To meet this situation, the planets which lie nearer the Sun must revolve more rapidly. We therefore find Mercury moving in its orbit at the rate of thirty-five miles per second, the Earth eighteen miles per second, Mars at fourteen miles per second, Jupiter at eight miles, Uranus at four, and Neptune at three.

Light, heat, sound, color, power, electricity, vegetation, health, sickness, all physical phenomena, the tides, wireless, and the radio are but manifestations of vibration and the various planets are immense masses of metal, gases, and chemicals which cause vibrations to which we respond, in much the same way as the loop aerial of the radio picks up the various stations.

As these planets change their relative position from time to time, the ratio of their vibrations changes, and certain vibrations grow stronger while others decrease.

For this reason, with the first breath that you took, every fiber on your being became impregnated with magnetic influences, and that personality is stamped upon you indelibly for all time, subtle vibrations always manifesting in exact accordance with the location of the various planets and the consequent vibrations existing in the ether at the moment of birth.

Thus it is that the scientist, knowing the exact hour of birth, the location, and the date, is able to calculate with an amount of accuracy limited only by his personal knowledge and experience, the exact positions of the planets and give a judgment therefrom.

As all change is the result of motion, there are three movements to be considered.

First, the revolution of the Earth around the Sun. This is completed in one year.

Second, the revolution of the Moon around the Earth. This is completed in one month.

Third, the rotation of the Earth upon its axis. This is completed in one day.

The cycle of the revolution of the Earth around the Sun is its Zodiac. In this cycle then are four seasons as the Earth enters the four Cardinal Signs: Aries about March 21st, Cancer about June 21st, Libra about September 21st, and Capricorn about December 21st.

The four points of sunrise, noon, sunset, and midnight are positions of marked change, because they indicate when one influence, or combination of influences, ends and another begins.

Day begins at sunrise, so that the sign or constellation which is on the ascendant or first zone at the commencement of your life, has within it all of the possibilities which can be subsequently manifested, just as the future course of a stone is determined by the amount of energy imparted to it by the hand when it is thrown into the air.

The next critical point is noon. Here the sun has attained it highest position, the energy which began at the sunrise has reached its culmination. This position at birth represents power, achievement, authority, dignity, elevation, publicity, fame, and honor.

The third division is sunset, which represents the polar opposite of sunrise. These two points are a pair of balanced opposites and represent similar conditions.

The fourth point is midnight. It represents seclusion, rest, the time when the psychic and astral influences are strongest.

Astronomically, the mass of the Sun is stated as about 700 times that of all its planets put together.

The Zodiac with all its infinite possibilities is the path of the Sun as seen from our earth; and the planets are specialized centres of that energy of which the Sun is the source and fountain head.

The Solar fluid is the ethereal atmosphere, or the ether, and is limited to the solar system; it is the medium for the transmissions of the potencies distributed by the various planets, and holds in solution the basic elements of all life and thought.

This ether is the only possible fluid which is sufficiently subtle to carry the delicate vibrations which are constantly being broadcasted over the radio, and which penetrate iron, wood, steel, and every other barrier, and which are not limited by either time or space.

Thus, we find that not only the Sun, but Venus, Mars, Saturn, the Moon, and all of the other planets radiate their own peculiar characteristics. This influence in turn is reflected in the character of those who come under the influence of these vibrations.

As the nature of the energy that the Sun radiates is in accordance with its intrinsic nature, so the nature of vibrations sent out by the planets are in accordance with their intrinsic natures.

Venus has long been regarded as the God of Love, consequently the characteristics of those coming under her influence are affectionate, sympathetic, refined, and contented. Mars has long been known as the God of War, and his influence is therefore courageous, venturesome, aggressive, and fearless; the influence of the Moon is reflective, receptive, and productive; of Mercury, intellectual, accomplished, skillful, and clever; of Jupiter, generous, philanthropic, moral, charitable, and sincere; of Saturn, prudent, cautious, patient, and reserved; of Uranus, original, ingenious, talented, and intuitive; of Neptune, idealistic, mystical, inspirational, and peculiar.

Each planet has its own rate of vibrations and its influence upon the earth depends upon the angle which it forms, certain angles causing the vibrations to be accelerated or diminished, magnified or retarded.

These angles of planetary influence have been found to produce effects just as certain and definite as the various angles in chemistry.

Thus the seven planets give the seven rays or vibrations or tunes, and the earth is the organ upon which these notes are played, and the harmony or inharmony resulting therefrom is the influence that we call good or evil, as the effect is pleasing or the reverse.

There are seven nerve plexi located at intervals along the spinal cord. The plexi correspond and act as service stations for the Seven Norms. They are:

sacral	–	Saturn
prostatic	–	Jupiter
epigastric or solar	–	Mars
cardiac	–	Sun
pharyngeal	–	Venus
laryngeal	–	Mercury
cavernous	–	Moon

These are the media for the diffusion of the astral essences, from which they are transmitted by the sympathetic nervous system to the various cells of the body for transmutation and assimilation.

A celestial impingement, therefore, never fails to express itself in the mental and physical plane of the ego.

The solar orb is the principle of life. It radiates pure being only. It is therefore Unity. Unity proceeds to diversity by a definite geometrical process.

As the planets revolve around the Sun, they radiate magnetism, the kind and character depending upon the nature of the planet. This magnetism in turn produces chemical and spiritual changes in accordance with the various combinations that are formed as the planets move in their accustomed orbits in the Zodiac.

The combination of zinc and copper does not create electricity, they only bring to a point of individualism that which exists everywhere. Likewise the planets are merely gigantic batteries moving in space.

Therefore, when Jupiter, which represents the principle of tin, comes into aspect with Venus, which represents the principle of copper, the vibrations which are produced in the celestial magnetism will be in accordance with the polarities which these planets possess at the time of such combination; or when Saturn, which represents the principle of lead and is therefore cold and negative, comes into a correlative aspect with the Sun, which represents the principle of Gold and is, therefore, dynamic and hot, there will be a vast disturbance in the vibratory influence and this inharmony will affect the life force of all who come under the influence of either of these heavenly bodies.

All impulses which manifest, and many more which do not manifest, through the senses find their original stimulus and direction in planetary vibrations. Life as we know it, originates, exists, and manifests through vibrations.

As the planets transit along their orbits through the Zodiac they form vibratory aspects to which we respond, each person responding according to his ability.

The planetary vibrations of varying character are continually exerting influence of which we may be entirely unconscious.

We find planetary action giving direction to metabolism, expanding, contracting, and otherwise changing the quality of bodily feelings which induce attitudes of mind—the attitude determining the course or character of our acts, which in turn make up our environment.

It must be remembered that we are not conscious of all our bodily reactions to stimuli; nor is every stimulus transformed into conscious thought. In fact, most of our bodily reactions are performed unconsciously.

There is a direct relation between the mind and matter. The higher branches of thought have their origin in the higher organs of the brain, and these are allied to the planets farthest from the Sun; while the lower branches of thought, as of facts and things, domestic affairs, money matters, etc., have their origin in the base of the brain and these are allied to the planets nearest the Sun.

For the nearer the Sun we get, the more active the planets are, and those persons who are influenced by them are correspondingly more active.

Whether we deal with Venus as a celestial body or as the unifying principle of Love, of Saturn as the essence of form or the sponsor of fear, of Mars as the element of energy or as the dynamic principle of courage, we must recognize the identity of specific conditions and grasp the comprehensive statement that the Universal Mind, though synthetic in essence, is manifested in infinite and complex form.

Light is good in whatever
    lamp it is burning.

A rose is beautiful in whatever
    garden it may bloom.

A star has the same radiance if
    it shine from the East or West.

Abdul Baha

A Book About You

Section Two

Solar Vibrations

In Revelations we are told, "And there were seven lamps of fire burning before the throne, which are the seven spirits of God." These lamps, burning before the throne, are the seven planets of our solar system.

These seven spirits are eternally involving and evolving the seven active Principles of the Universe.

Each planet has its own particular individual physical force and this physical force exerts a spiritual influence in accordance with the nature of the individuality in the family of planets. Saturn radiates substance of form, Jupiter radiates power or expression, Mars radiates energy or courage, Venus radiates harmony or love, Mercury radiates intelligence or mind, Uranus radiates genius or intuition, Neptune radiates spiritual causation or inspiration.

Here then are the seven immense power houses generating and radiating all that is, all that ever was or ever can be. With the seven basic notes or tones every possible combination of music can be made, so with these seven primal forces every possible combination can be brought about.

Your ability to express, is therefore, simply your ability to absorb.

You can give only in proportion as you are enabled to receive—no more, no less.

You can draw forth that which you have the capacity to discern.

You can adjust your self to those planes of existence only of which you are conscious.

This is rue upon all planes of existence: physical, mental, moral, or spiritual.

Your physical sensations depend upon your degree of sensitiveness.

Your sympathies go to those who can appreciate your motives.

You are in harmony with those only who are upon your plane of intellectual comprehension.

You appreciate the morale of others only as your own understanding has been awakened.

The principle of Saturn is manifest in scholars, philosophers, priests, hermits, all such melancholy and reserved persons who lead a solitary and retired life and are more disposed to contemplation than to action; but as contemplation precedes action and as thought precedes speech, so the merchant, the manufacturer, the banker are all dependent upon the contemplation of the inventor, the artisan, and the architect; likewise, the statesman and the orator receive their ideas and policies from the philosopher, the one finding and the other executing.

By virtue of their organic structure, the planetary orbs are gigantic batteries through which spiritual energies seek manifestation. They represent principles which coexist throughout all forms of material expression.

The same mind which incites the planet in its mutation to form certain aspects affects every action in a corresponding ration, because every atom is a concrete expression of spiritual energy and is endowed with magnetic responsiveness in perfect accord with certain activities which constitute its Divine harmony. The planetary complexion of the heavens at birth may therefore be accepted as the correct measurement of your psychical value in the Universal economy.

For this reason, your ego, upon the moment of birth, attracted those influences only that are in harmony with your spiritual requirements.

This does not necessarily imply fatalism or predestination because you partake of the nature of the whole, and are consequently potentially limitless. For this reason if you have a clear knowledge of the astral conditions which surround you, you may relate with those which are constructive and desirable and repulse those which might bring about adverse conditions; while on the other hand if you have no knowledge of the conditions that the celestial orbits are providing, you will drift blindly and consequently may be entirely unprepared to successfully cope with conditions when they arrive.

As the various celestial bodies are constantly sending forth emanations which must necessarily correspond with their character, all space holds in suspension not only all of these characteristics, but the new characteristics both of the chemical changes caused by the combination and absorption of the emanation of two or more bodies.

Thus, the influences that reach you and to which you respond are magnetic influences caused by the various combinations of the celestial bodies as the pass and repass in their various orbits.

The Cosmos contains the sum and substance of the essence of all the celestial bodies, and this essence contains the totality of Being, and as a part cannot disassociate itself from the whole, every individual must necessarily partake of these characteristics.

Saturn represents the formative principle.

Jupiter represents the spiritual principle.

Mars represents the aggressive principle.

Sun represents the vital principle.

Venus represents the love principle.

Mercury represents the intellectual principle.

Moon represents the emotional principle.

These are the seven norms which are active in every impulse and which constitute the Divine essence which enters into and becomes the virtues as well as the faults, and graces as well as the perversions of all organic life; they are responsible for every manifestation of form throughout the mineral, the vegetable, or the animal kingdom.

At birth you were a drop out of the ocean of the universe, and, as such, are chemically identical with that ocean at the time of extraction.

As every atom in the universe is a concrete expression of spiritual energy and is endowed with a magnetic responsiveness to the activities which constitute Divine harmony, the vital moment is the psychic key by which you may ascertain the exact relationship which you bear to the whole.

From iron to steel and then to gold is the stairway you must climb. Life is a progress, life is earnest, life is real—and you must either refine your life or delay your progress.

The Earth turns on its axis once in twenty-four hours. It is clear, then, that it will pass the whole circle of the Zodiac once each day. This circle of the Zodiac through which the Earth passes each day has been divided into twelve zones.

These zones represent the limitations or opportunities appertaining to your daily life, while the celestial signs relate to the sum total of you experiences. The planets represent the causes which alternately remove or establish conditions and experiences.

The first zone governs your environment, your disposition, and your self-interests—in a word, your personality.

The second zone governs your financial affairs and monetary prospects.

The third zone, your relatives, travel, and the general state of your objective mind.

The fourth zone, your residence, your home life, your parents, and the conditions at the close of life.

The fifth zone, your social affairs, your love affairs, and your children.

The sixth zone, your health, your employes, and your psychic tendencies.

The seventh zone, your marriage or business partner and your individual qualities—in a word, your individuality.

The eighth zone, wills, legacies in which you may be interested.

The ninth zone, long journeys, foreign affairs and the general state of your subjective mind.

The tenth zone, your profession, honors and ambitions, and mental and moral conditions generally.

The eleventh zone, your ability to make friends and acquaintances.

The twelfth zone, unseen troubles and misfortunes, emotional tendencies.

So far as the physical plane is concerned, the twelve divisions of the ecliptic called zones may be regarded as powers brought into activity by the influence of the Sun upon the Earth. They are all differentiations of cosmic force acting in the earth's aura and kept active by the vibrations set in motion by the Sun and differentiated by the various planets as shown in the following table:

	Metal	Color	Control	Manifests as
Sun	Gold	Orange	Heart	Spirit
Moon	Silver	Green	Brain	Soul
Mercury	Quicksilver	Violet	Lungs	Intellect
Venus	Copper	Yellow	Veins	Love
Mars	Iron	Red	Gall	Energy
Jupiter	Tin	Indigo	Liver	Judgement
Saturn	Lead	Blue	Spleen	Memory

It will be seen why the rays of the Sun are capable of refraction in the seven prismatic colors.

The principle of Venus is the same, be it expressed as love in the human emotions, or as the active basis of copper in the metallic kingdom; it will always respond to kindred vibrations.

The principle of Mercury is intelligence or mind. As the luminiferous ether is impregnated by the archetypal ideas, so does Mercury enter into and quicken the sulphurous property of the material principal in you, which is significant of the intellect—the restless reaching out for the unattainable, the unfoldment of the aspirations of your soul.

The influence of Jupiter makes you magnanimous, generous, fond of learning, a lover of outdoor sports.

If Venus is the impinging force, you will be loving, kind, and possibly sensual; all depending upon the dignity of the planet at the time of nativity.

If Saturn is your ruling planet you will be patient, reserved, and economical.

The characteristics which the vibrations from the planets stimulate may be summarized as follows:

Mars: impulsive, courageous, aggressive, active, perceptive, impatient, and contentious.

Venus: loving, amiable, affectionate, charitable, sensuous, fond of pleasure, artistic, and sociable.

Mercury: imaginative, studious, sharp, witty, persuasive, logical, and oratorical.

Sun: noble, generous, faithful and sincere, ambitious and proud.

Moon: receptive, mutable, impressionable, changeable, yet refined and ingenious.

Jupiter: generous, noble and sincere, compassionate and religious, courteous, just, honorable, prudent, and faithful.

Saturn: perceptive, apprehensive, economical, reserved, constant and patient, laborious, reflective, and innately chaste.

Uranus: original, abrupt, erratic, romantic, bohemian or metaphysical turn of mind and antiquarian tastes.

Neptune: psychic, emotional, romantic, plastic, dreamy, innately mystical, and indifferent to worldly matters.

It is apparent that your temperament, disposition, and personality will depend upon in which of the zones your ruling planet is found.

You may wonder why the Sun in the first zone at birth will bring long life, honor, and vitality; or Mercury in the second zone brings success in literary and scientific pursuits; why should Mars in the first zone endow one with a distinguished appearance and martial bearing; why should Venus in the tenth zone indicate a brilliant and successful marriage; why should Jupiter in the fourth zone indicate success in real estate operations; and why should Saturn in the same zone indicate loss in the same business?

The reply is, why, if the brain be disturbed in a certain zone, will the memory be affected; if it be disturbed in another zone, why will the sense of sight be affected; in still another, why will the ability to reason be destroyed?

The brain consists of a large number of nerve fibres and power does not consist in their number or size of the strings alone, but upon the length; and so the character of the vibration, and this wave length depends upon the station or zone from which it is broadcast.

And finally, it must never be forgotten, that Science is empirical, results depend upon experimentation. A physician will not tell one that by cutting away a certain part of the brain the memory will be destroyed, until this has been found to be true by actual experimentation; and likewise, statements concerning the resultant activities of the planets in the various zones are not theories or guess work, but the result of actual knowledge derived by observation through thousands and thousands of experiences which have taken hundreds of years to secure and classify; and what is still more interesting, such information may be verified by any one at any time, for you may easily secure a natal chart and watch the effects of the planets as they transit the zones. If you do this, you will never again doubt the effect of Jupiter on your financial affairs, or of Venus upon your social and love affairs.

The greater the difficulty,
The more glory in the surmounting it;
Skillful pilots gain their reputation,
From storms and tempests.

—Epicurus

Section Three

Mental Vibrations

Energy reveals itself in manifold phases according to the media through which it manifests. The energy is one and identical, but it becomes diversified as it penetrates different substances or organisms. Infinite energy is ether in motion, or rhythmic vibration. Consciousness, then, is the registration of the Universal Energy within a vital organism.

When the Earth is turned toward the Sun, the direct rays agitate the nerve cells of the body. This agitation or vibration results in what we term consciousness.

All nerve cells possess dendrites which touch each other and by means of which nerve currents are transmitted from one cell to another. These currents are necessary for consciousness and when the dendrites no longer contact these direct rays or currents, they spontaneously grow shorter so that they no longer come in contact with one another and sleep results. The neurons simply draw in their processes at night. To use a popular phrase, they "hang up the receiver."

The sensory stimuli that reach us during sleep are not of a nature or an intensity to arouse conscious vibrations, but they often give rise to dreams. Dreams of this type are illusions pure and simple, such as are not unusual in normal life and which are so common in many of the neuroses. They are simply the erroneous interpretation of actual stimuli.

The universe is regarded as composed of several regions or planes, of which our visible physical plane is one. The Earth and everything in it—with the Sun, Moon, and planets—are situated on the physical plane. The other planes are not distant globes removed from us by space, but are situated in the "within" of space, everywhere surrounding and interpenetrating the planes we know.

To distinguish these interior planes, the expedient seems to have been accepted from the very ancient times of naming them after the states of matter with which we are familiar: earth, water or air.

These three forms of consciousness correspond to the three relative rates of motion: the Sun, the Moon, and the Earth. The Earth turns upon its axis in one day. During this time it contacts all twelve of the great constellations, remaining in each one for a period of two hours. We thus receive every celestial vibration and consequential state of consciousness.

Every human being is essentially a spark of the "Divine Light", the light that lighteth every man that cometh into the world, the Divine spark that can reach the matrix of matter only by coming into contact with the physical plane or denser region of the material world. The unit of consciousness is a seed placed in the material world that is constantly turning and in a day of twenty four hours comes under the influence of all the constellations. In Taurus, the sense of smell is developed. In Gemini, the sense of touch is developed. In Cancer, the sense of taste is developed. In Leo, the sense of sight is developed. In Virgo and Libra, the internal organs of the brain are developed. In Scorpio, the generative forces are quickened.

Having now acquired all of his physical sense, man turns to Sagittarius where he is imbued with the qualities of love and devotion. He is then carried to Capricorn, the symbol of action and service. Next comes Aquarius from which he receives reason and intuition, and finally he is placed under the influence of Pisces where he is given wisdom and understanding.

Mind is a phase of transformed energy in every form of organic matter. It is in the molecule as well as in the cell. This energy, impinging on the elements that compose the substances of the earth, is transformed into the molecular energy that maintains and organizes physical substances, namely adhesion and cohesion. This is mind in germinal form, for the office of molecular energy is creative and to that extent implies a reaction in the molecule that is the basis of thought and feeling.

The evolution of life from organic materials is only one state more mysterious than the evolution of any from of matter from another, for in fact it is of that type and the new changes are little more startling than those that occur at other levels in the chain of creation.

Every human being is a microcosmos within himself. He is a universe of cells, each with its individual intelligence. Within his universe, these cells, countless in number, are dying by millions almost momentarily. The cast off physical bodies of the cells are thrown out of the human system in waste. The life spark in each cell immediately reincarnates and does so over and over again as long as the human system lasts. The intelligence of all the cells makes up the sum total of the intelligence of the human system.

Man has been deficient in understanding because his brain receiver did not vibrate to certain subtle influences; the dynamic cell in gray matter of nerve was not finely attuned and did not respond.

The situation may be illustrated by a tuning fork, which may be taken to represent individual or personal consciousness. The fork is in tune B flat. Place it on the piano and run the scales up and down without sounding B flat and the tuning fork is unresponsive. Let the B flat be sounded, to which the tuning fork is in harmony and immediately the fork vibrates. All the notes on the piano are non-existent to the tuning fork except the one with which it is in accord.

Call the tones sounded by the piano suggestions. The only suggestion that has any influence over the tuning fork in the one with which its own pitch is in accord. It is not the piano, but the pitch of the tuning fork, which determines whether or not the tuning fork shall vibrate. Nor does the tuning fork vibrate because it happens to be near some particular piano and is affected by that piano's peculiarities. Let the B flat be sounded on a violin, or on a tin pan for that matter, and the tuning fork will vibrate just as readily. The power given to the suggestion is not in the instrument, but in the pitch of the tuning fork.

Suppose that someone should desire to destroy the susceptibility of the tuning fork to the pitch of B flat, seeing that the tuning fork vibrates when B flat is struck on the piano—what would be more natural than for him to conclude that the piano alone is responsible for the behavior of the tuning fork, and from this premise to reason that by taking away the piano or removing the tuning fork from the sphere of the piano's influence, the desired end will be accomplished and the tuning fork will no longer be affected by B flat. Nothing would be accomplished by such procedures, for the reasoning is from the erroneous premise. The susceptibility of the tuning fork to B flat has nothing to do with the environment, and no manipulation of the environment can have any effect. There is just one way to make the tuning fork unresponsive to B flat, and that is to change its pitch.

Personal consciousness is like the tuning fork. It has a certain pitch. This pitch is given at the moment of birth and the elements that go to make up its peculiar nature determine its points of susceptibility to suggestion. The great range of possible suggestions under the classifications of heredity and environment, personality, or race will mean nothing to the personal consciousness unless the elements or qualities are presented which appeal to this particular consciousness as real. Then personal sense will respond by accepting the suggestion and manifesting the characteristics of the suggestion.

There is a plane of thought constituting the animal plane. Here are the actions and interactions that animals respond to, yet men know nothing of. Then we have the conscious thought plane. Here are almost limitless planes of thought to which we may be responsive. It is strictly the nature of our thinking that determine to which plane we shall respond. On this plane, we have the thoughts of the ignorant, the wise, the poor, and so on. The number of thought planes is infinite, but the point is that when we think on a definite plane, we are responsive to thoughts on that plane and the effect of the reaction on that plane in our environment.

Consciousness is positive, active, changeful, and outgoing; and activity, will in action, volition, and conation are terms applicable to it. In many cases it is only a reaction on the part of the environment; for instance food is part of the environment, and its rejection is a reaction against the environment. This is sometimes called will, but it is not the same as the metaphysical will, which is controlled from within, influenced by attractions and repulsions in the environment.

Relation, therefore, is the essence of this aspect of consciousness; and just as action may be of two kinds—to separate and to bring together—and just as feelings may be of two kinds—agreeable and disagreeable—so there may be two kinds of relation, those of similarity and dissimilarity.

It is evident that the actions that separate, feelings that are disagreeable, and relations of dissimilarity are all obviously separative, individualizing, and correspond to the downward arc; while actions that unite, feelings that are agreeable, and relations that are of similarity are integrative and upbuilding.

Around you, as the center of it, the world without revolves. Organized life, people, thoughts, sounds, light, the universe itself with its numberless millions of phenomena are sending out vibrations toward you: vibrations of love, of hate, thoughts good and bad, wise and unwise, true and untrue.

These vibrations are directed toward you—by the smallest as well as by the greatest, the farthest and the nearest. A few of them reach you but the rest pass by, and as far as you are concerned lost.

Some of these vibrations are essential to your health, your power, your success, your happiness. How is it that they pass you?

Luther Burbank[1] said: "We are just beginning to realize what a wonderful machine is the human brain. We are at the threshold of knowledge, but until yesterday we were outside. The human race has been broadcasting and receiving, perhaps millions of years without knowing, but suffering all the while from bad thoughts sent. The radio, while but a very simple instrument as compared to the brain, is helping us to understand what the brain has always been doing.

---

[1] Luther Burbank (1849-1926) was a widely known botanist and scientist who earned fame in breeding new fruits, plants, and flowers. He was also an iconoclast and freethinker.

"Those who are familiar with the radio know what jamming means—the crowding into a narrow wave-belt of a great many sending stations, all operating at once. Since we are all transmitting every time we think, it is obvious that the jamming in wave-length belts used by radio transmitters is as nothing compared with the din made by a billion and a half human brains. Din may seem to be a strange word to use in connection with the ether over a quiet meadow, for instance, but those who know how to operate radio receiving sets will understand. No matter how much jamming is going on, a radio receiving set is as the grave until it is adjusted and made resonant by establishing harmony within it. The silence may then change into what may seem to be almost screaming.

"With everybody broadcasting at once it follows that the ether must be the sounding chamber into which is crowded every kind of human thought. As we do not broadcast with the same intensity, it follows that the weaker vibrations must be drowned out by the stronger ones. Weak thoughts must soon fall flat, while strong ones may go to the ends of the earth. But it seems logical to believe that thoughts, held in common by millions, may, because of their identical nature, swell into a tremendous chorus, even though the human transmitters may not individually be very strong senders."

We easily recognize three phases of consciousness between each of which there are enormous differences.

1. **Simple Consciousness,** which all animals possess in common. It is the sense of existence, by which we recognize that "we are" and "that we are where we are" and by which we perceive the various objects and varied scenes and conditions.

2. **Self Consciousness,** possessed by all mankind, except infants and the mentally deficient. This gives the power of self contemplation, the effect of the world without upon our world within. "Self contemplates self." Amongst many other results, language has thus come into existence, each word being a symbol for a thought or an idea.

3. **Cosmic Consciousness.** This form of consciousness is as much above self-consciousness as self-consciousness is above the simple consciousness. It is as different from either as sight is different from hearing or touch.

Neither by simple consciousness nor by self-consciousness can one get any notion of cosmic-consciousness. It is not like either of them any more than sight is like hearing. A deaf man can never learn of the value of music by means of his sense of sight or touch.

Cosmic consciousness is all forms of consciousness. It overrides time and space, for apart from the body and the world of matter, these do not exist.

The immutable law of consciousness is: *That in the degree that the consciousness is developed so is the development of power in the subjective and its consequent manifestation in the objective.*

Cosmic consciousness is the result of the creation of the necessary conditions so that the Universal Mind may function in the direction desired.

If you do not seem to grasp the application of the law of vibration in the thought world, if you do not know how to change the rate of vibration, remember that every thought changes the rate of vibration. As you think greater, deeper, higher, and more forceful thoughts, the brain cells are refined, they become more powerful, and they are enabled to receive finer vibrations.

This is true not only in the mental world but in the physical world. As the ear becomes trained in music, it is enabled to receive finer vibrations until the trained musician can hear harmonies of sound of which the ordinary person is entirely unaware.

Planetary vibrations act chiefly upon the nervous system, which is governed by, or responsive to, the planet of Mercury. The nervous system is the messenger of the mind and through the mind is transmitted the intelligent impulses which know how to direct the actions of the various organs of the body so as to bring about appropriate responses in the organs selected and the functions involved.

If you wish to be strong, the subconscious mind acts upon the tendency indicated and you will unconsciously do those things which will manifest strength. Every thought finds expression in the degree of its monopoly, hence, if you very much want and desire strength you must give the thoughts of strength form, purpose, and power—you must give the thought of strength a monopoly.

The general principle by which an idea is preserved is vibratory like all other phenomena of nature. Every thought causes a vibration that will continue to expand and contract in wave circles, like the waves started by a stone dropped in a pool of water. Waves from other thoughts may counteract it, or it may finally succumb of its own inanition.

Subconscious thought is received by any organ of the body affected, and think of the mechanism with which you are provided and which can and does objectify the thought received. First the millions of cell chemists ready and waiting to carry out all instructions received. Next the complete system of communication, consisting of the vast sympathetic nervous system reaching every fibre of the being and ready to respond to the slightest emotion of joy or fear, of hope or despair, of courage or impotence.

Next the complete manufacturing plant consisting of the series of glands wherein are manufactured all the secretions necessary for the use of the chemists in carrying our the instructions which are given.

Then the complete digestive tract wherein food, water, and air are converted into blood, bone, skin, hair, and nails.

Finally, the supply department which constantly sends a supply of oxygen, nitrogen, and ether into every part of the being, and the wonder of it all is that this ether holds in solution everything necessary for the use of the chemist, for the ether holds in pure form—and food, water, and air in secondary form—every element necessary for the production of a perfect individual.

You are also provided with a complete equipment for the elimination of waste and useless material as well as a complete repair department. In a addition to this, you have a complete system of wireless whereby you are connected with every other subconscious entity in existence.

You are not usually conscious of the operation of this wireless, but the same thing is true concerning the operation of the Marconi System.

There may be music of every kind in the air, but unless you make use of the amplifier, you receive no message and so with your subconscious wireless. Unless you try to co-ordinate the conscious and subconscious, you fail to realize that the subconscious is constantly receiving messages of some kind and just as constantly objectifying the message in your life and environment.

Try the following exercise:

Lie down quietly. Relax completely your mind and body. Breathe naturally. If the mind is at all tense or strained, then results cannot be obtained.

The mind must relax for the flow of inspiration.

Sooner or later there will be a warm, magnetic sensation throughout the body. As you progress you will lose the sense of the body altogether. The breathing will grow less in volume. Finally the conscious breath will cease.

You will be in the Silence; you can go where you please and return at will. You may roam in mind through the subjective world of thought.

You will be in tune with the cosmic consciousness.

You will be in tune with the Infinite.

YOU

You are whole perfect, strong and powerful.

You are unfettered, unbound, triumphant and victorious!

You are youthful, vigorous, smiling, buoyant and splendid.

You are active, energetic, lively, independent and sagacious.

You are loyal, tactful, alert, contented and considerate.

You are renewed, regenerated, recreated, inspired and transformed.

You are refreshed, invigorated, loving, harmonious and happy—yes, wondrously happy.

You have found the elixir of life—the philosopher's stone—the life abundant—the fountain of youth.

Section Four
Electrical Vibrations

The only important theory that has ever been advanced to explain the properties of electricity is that of Faraday[1]; which theory is that the region surrounding charged bodies is traversed by lines of force, the ends of which are rigidly attached to bodies charged with electricity of opposite polarities.

Lodge[2] regards the electron as a point charge of disembodied electricity and nothing else, the vibrating corpuscle being a constituent of the atom but itself possessing no material nucleus. He is responsible for the theory that all matter is electrical in nature and there are now no physical scientists who doubt the truth of the constitution of matter in accordance with this theory.

The earth is a huge magnet electrified by the sun and the impulse, sensations, and varied states of consciousness of every living things depend upon the vibrations which are constantly being received from the planets. The planets too are huge magnets but of varying sizes and of different constitutions, each of which is likewise electrified by the sun.

If a copper wire be bound spirally around a bar of soft iron and an electric current passed through the wire, the bar of iron will, for the time being, be converted into a magnet. If the bar with its spirally wound wire be balanced on a point or hung horizontally on a thread

---

[1] Michael Faraday (1791-1867) is often regarded as the greatest experimentalist in the history of science. He was a physicist and a chemist. In 1845, he discovered what is today called the Faraday Effect about which he wrote, "I have at last succeeded in illuminating a magnetic curve or line of force and in magnetising a ray of light."

[2] Sir Oliver Joseph Lodge (1851-1940) was an English physicist who contributed to many fields, including radio, elctron research, and chemistry. His most famous books was *Modern Views of Electricity*, written in 1889. Lodge devoted the later years of his life to psychical research.

so that it can swing around, it will point north and south like a permanent magnet or a magnet needle.

An empty spiral of wire, one with no bar passing through it, will behave in exactly the same way if an electric current is sent along the wire and it is balanced so that it can swing. It will point north and south as long as the current passes and the end that points south will be the one at which the current is travelling around the spiral in the same direction as the hands of a watch.

In magnetism, like poles repel each other and unlike poles attract. The north pole of a magnet will repel the north pole of a magnetic needle, but will attract the south pole of the needle.

Because the needle is a permanent magnet, the obvious inference from the fact of its pointing north and south is that the magnetism at the north pole of the earth must be similar in its nature and in the direction of its electric currents to that at the south-pointing end of the needle or of a bar magnet. Magnetic attraction implies opposites; therefore the magnetism at the north pole of the earth must be opposite in nature to that of the north-pointing end of the magnet. In fact, the earth behaves as if a great bar magnet were thrust through its axis; the south pole of the magnet being at the north pole of the earth.

It follows from this that electric currents are travelling spirally around the earth from pole to pole. If we could look down upon the north pole of the earth and could see these currents, they would appear to move in the same direction as the hands of a watch; that is to say, they would behave just as do the sun, moon, and planets—rise in the east, pass across the meridian, and set in the west.

All electrical energy has its source in the Sun, which is the center of all life, force, and energy, and represents the positive and primal fount of all existence. In the sun are contained all the colors of the solar spectrum. Every form of existence manifesting in the solar system is bathed in these rays from which is drawn the life that is at the center of its existence.

The Moon represents the negative influence, her light being that which is borrowed from the Sun, she having no light of her own except that which she collects as a reflector.

We may think of the Sun as the symbol of the spirit and the Moon of matter, the two acting in unison as spirit matter, or life and form.

The planets nearest the Sun are most active in motion. Making their revolutions around the Sun in the shortest length of time, they travel through space at the greatest rate of speed. As we recede from the Sun toward the orbit of Neptune, this activity of the planets becomes gradually less. Thus mercury travels through space at the rate of 29.3 miles per second and accomplishes a revolution around the Sun in about eighty-seven days; while Neptune, the farthest removed of the planets, has a velocity of about three and one-half miles a second and requires about 165 years to make a revolution around the Sun. Our Earth travels at the rate of nineteen miles a second or seventy-five times faster than a cannon ball.

Mercury is about 3000 miles in diameter or approximately three-eights the diameter of the Earth. Its mean distance from the Sun is 35,393,000 miles. Its orbit is the most elliptical of all the planets, sometimes approaching within 28,153,000 miles of the Sun and at other times removed 42,669,000 miles.

It is by nature convertible, being affected by the planet with which it is in conjunction. When apart from any other influence, Mercury is a changeable, cold, dry, and "mercurial" planet.

Those who are born under its influence are extremely sensitive to the rise and fall in atmospheric pressure. The body is easily affected by environment, and is therefore liable to feelings of comfort and discomfort according to circumstances. Physically, Mercury governs the brain, nerves, bowels, arms and hands, mouth, tongue, and lungs. The temperament is excitable, very quick and active, rather changeable, and sometimes highly nervous.

Mercury has been termed "the Messenger of the Gods" and he seems to have the special office of being the messenger of every other planet to the Sun. He is the great mental ruler, for without Mercury's influence we should be devoid of memory and probably of speech, and also all other power of expression.

Mercury is therefore the great actor in life's drama.

The orbit of Venus, like that of Mercury, lies within the orbit of the Earth; and, like Mercury, she is sometimes an evening and sometimes a morning star. Her orbit is larger than that of Mercury, but it never recedes more than 48 degrees from the Sun.

Venus accomplishes one sidereal revolution in about 225 days. The diameter of Venus is 7,510 miles; its distance from the Sun is 66,586,000 miles.

Venus is the most beautiful planet in the solar system[1]. Her influence is for pleasure, cheerfulness and affection.

Venus is decidedly a feminine planet, presiding over all affairs which concern females, and the clinging preserving, nourishing and sustaining element; therefore she has the greatest influence in feminine affairs. She brings out all of the artistic, idealistic, and musical faculties. She presides over the higher emotions and refined desires, as well as over the sensuous feelings. Sentiment and pleasurable desires govern the Venus nature, and wherever mirth, pleasure and joy are found the vibrations from Venus has a decided influence of her own. She is also affected by the aspects from other planets, the feelings and emotions being depressed or expanded according to the nature of the planet with which she is in aspect.

The typical Venus woman is well developed in every way, of medium stature and beautiful skin. The complexion is clear and attractive, the eyes very bright and sparkling, inclined to be dark blue or hazel, and full of feeling. The colour of the eyes and hair is affected by the

---

[1] One must keep in mind that when Haanel is describing these planets, he is referring to how they have been traditionally described and also what was known about them at the time. To this day, Venus appears in the sky brilliant and beautiful to the naked eye; but, that has nothing to do with the fact that Venus is a lifeless planet with an atmosphere composed primarily of carbon dioxide and surface temperatures as high as 932° F.

planets aspecting Venus. The face is smiling and pleasant, the voice soft and sweet. The pure Venus type woman is irresistible in charm and she seems destined to draw out all the love and affection of those around her.

Physically, Venus confers beauty of form, clearness of skin, fine hair, and firm flesh, which is usually healthy.

Mentally, she confers an appreciation of the fine arts, but gives very little inclination for study or intellectual pursuits, those born under her influence being more guided by their feelings than by thought or reason. The moral qualities are sometimes rather latent, the Venus temperament preferring to obtain its desires quickly and easily by the most convenient methods and strict morality, or sometimes even reason, is often disregarded where these desires are in question.

The Venus disposition is cheerful, merry, generous, light-hearted, and sometimes very witty. Males born under Venus are affable, courteous, kind, and sympathetic, though sometimes rather effeminate. Venus governs the feelings and emotions only, and these feelings and emotions will be affected by the planets aspecting or influencing Venus at the time of birth.

Mars is the first of the superior planets; and by superior is meant that it orbit lies outside the orbit of the Earth.

Mars rotates on its axis in twenty-four hours and thirty-seven minutes, and accomplishes a revolution around the Sun in about six weeks less than two years.

The planet Mars is by nature hot and expansive, his influence being entirely different from that of Venus. The latter governs all that is gentle, soft, and feeling, whilst Mars governs all that is forceful, harsh, and often unfeeling. This planet is freer too from the influence of the other planets and distributes a more definite influence of his own, Mars being representative of the masculine sex in the same way that Venus is representative of the feminine sex. The Mars man is of medium height and stature, having a round face and ruddy complexion, sharp, bright eyes, often hazel, a good constitution and healthy body, and a splendid masculine system.

Physically, Mars governs the external generative system, the muscular system, as well as everything in the body connected with movement and action.

Mentally, Mars presides over all adventure, enterprise, and heroism. The influence of Mars is daring, combative, fearless, and venturesome. In everything where pluck, force, and energy are required, the Mars man will be foremost; always ready to defend, he will not hesitate to attack when the situation seems to require action.

The disposition of Mars men is generous, confident, and assertive; quickly angered, often acting rashly and ever inclined to be headstrong, they are first in any act of bravery, frequently regardless of consequences.

The next planet beyond the orbit of Mars is Jupiter.

To the naked eye, Jupiter appears as a star of the first magnitude. Its light is constant and scintillates but rarely. This giant planet is over 85,000 miles in diameter, or about 1,300 times larger than the Earth.

The circumference of Jupiter is 268,000 miles or more than ten times the circumference of our Earth.

Jupiter is universally known as the planet of good fortune. Every vibration of this planet is harmonious; and all those who have entered fully into the conditions of Jupiter are the essence of peace, morality, and justice, which last is combined with sympathy and compassion. All persons who come under the influence of this benefic planet are hopeful, joyous, sincere, truthful, and genuinely warm-hearted. Jupiterian individuals are marked by their sober, sincere, honest, and commanding appearances. They are of full stature, high forehead, and possess a luxuriant growth of hair. There is usually a display of true pride and dignity, which is never scornful or arrogant, but goes well with a nature that is benevolent and generous, anxious to do good and to benefit others.

The influence of Jupiter is manifested in prudent ambitions, in magnanimous action, and in sympathetic feelings for the good of humanity. The genuine Jupiterian is the most soft and gentle, and at the same time the most manly and noble of all dispositions. The most desirable virtues are to be found in this disposition; a noble nature, always acting honourably, ever grateful and genuinely courteous to all, high or low, one which is always happy, peaceful, and sincere.

Jupiter is the "greater fortune," the most benefic of planets. Without his influence, there would be no real joy. The vibrations of Jupiter bring bliss and a desire to be helpful.

Yet farther removed from the Sun is Saturn. Saturn is a planet differing in every way from any of the four we have so far considered. By nature, this planet is cold, limiting, restricting, and binding. Physically, Saturn presides over the bony structure. Those born under the influence of Saturn are usually lean, of middle stature, narrow forehead, small eyes, and pale complexion. The hair is usually very dark and sometimes black.

Mentally, Saturn governs the thoughtful, meditative tendencies, and makes the mind slow, careful, methodical, patient, contemplative, reserved, and studious.

Morally, Saturn gives justice and he favours all who are chaste, ascetic, pure-minded, frugal, and prudent.

In disposition, Saturnine persons are grave and sober, inclined to little speech, but giving expression to words of great weight when necessary. There is a tendency toward doubt and apprehension; but the disposition is inclined to be faithful and constant, reliable, industrious, and persevering.

Saturn turns on its axis in ten and one-half hours and requires nearly thirty years to complete a revolution around the Sun. The mean diameter of Saturn is about 70,100 miles, or 746 times larger than the Earth. It is 872,137,000 miles away and shines as a star of the first magnitude.

The planet Uranus strikes the highest octave to which we of the present are capable of responding. In fact, there are a great number of human beings who, as yet, are incapable of answering to the Uranus vibration. Its power is illustrated by those who today are not limited by conventional laws, but who maintain their own ideas free from personal bias and public opinion.

Physically, Uranus acts upon the nerves and the magnetic conditions. Surrounding everyone, there is what is called an aura, which is the magnetic field. Uranus governs that aura.

Intellectually, Uranus governs the inventive and ingenious faculties and favours the romantic, bohemian, and uncommon side of life, and all qualities that are unique and original, such as genius and intuition. This planet inclines toward metaphysical studies, or those principally concerned with the higher mind and the subjective parts of nature.

The disposition of those under Uranian influence is somewhat abrupt, inclined to be mystical, profound and gravely thoughtful, delighting in difficult problems, ancient mysteries, and occult sciences.

After Uranus had been discovered for some time, it was found that upon taking all known causes into account, there was still something affecting its motion. It was suggested that this something was another planet, more distant from the Sun than Uranus itself; and the question was, "Where was the planet if it existed?"

We need not be surprised that two minds, who felt themselves competent to solve the problem, should have independently undertaken to find the unknown world. As far back as July, 1841, we find Mr. Adams determined to investigate the irregularities of Uranus. Early in September, 1846, the new planet had been fairly grappled. We find Sir John Herschel remarking, "We see it as Columbus saw America from the shores of Spain. Its movements have been felt trembling along the far reaching line of our analysis with a certainty hardly inferior to ocular demonstration."

On the 29th of July, 1846, the large telescope of the Cambridge Observatory was first employed to search for the planet in the place where Professor Adams' calculations had assigned it. M. Le Verrier in September wrote to the Berlin observers stating the place where his calculations led him to believe it would be found, his theoretical place and Professor Adams' being not a degree apart. At Berlin, thanks to their star map, which had not yet been published, Dr. Gallac found the planet very near the position assigned by both astronomers.

The intuitive faculty and the telepathic sense, as well as genius, are frequently of a nature which might be directly ascribed to the planet Neptune. Hence, it would appear to be in the nature of Neptune to augment and specialize the faculties.

We must not, however, forget that the planets, according to their several natures, always act in terms of ourselves and our environment. A man who is listless and without ambition will not make bold or successful enterprises under the transit of Mars. A man of small ideas will account himself lucky on the receipt of an unexpected dole. Great achievements can come only from great minds and high endeavours. Mars always exacts the penalty of a risk. Saturn demands time in which to mature his benefits. Jupiter is a planet of "great expectations," and oftentimes of little permanence. Neptune dearly loves a plot or intrigue, and Uranus can make or break, according as a man is himself disposed to be constructive or destructive. Man is an embodied universe. The planets are all compounded in his being. It is that which makes him responsive to their actions.

The seven planets are the indicators of the seven Principles which constitute the universe. Just as the Zodiac is complete within itself, with twelve divisions, so are the planets a complete whole in the aura of the Sun, with seven divisions.

As one ray coming from the Sun is broken up into seven rays through the planets, so is each of the seven again broken up into millions of separate rays, each one forming the nucleus for a separate form of matter.

Thus, all life is manifested by combining and compounding these planetary influences.

The story of the formation of the Earth and man has been likened to a mighty wheel ever slowly and inevitably turning, ever pressing onward, each revolution being called an Age. As this "wheel of life" turns, it carries both humanity and the Earth through the various changes and states of unfoldment of their interwoven, yet individual, destinies.

When the physical body is conceived, it is under the prevailing lunar influence. At the time of "quickening," Mars animates the body and the particular planet which is in the ascendant at the moment governs the brain and nervous system.

When a child draws its first breath, it draws into its system a wave of ether charges with certain vibrations coming from the planetary spheres.

Every human being is essentially a seed of the Divine Life, and the unfoldment of the spiritual life within is the one aim of human destiny.

All planetary forces reaching our globe affect us physically, emotionally, and intellectually through our physical, emotional, and mental bodies. The principle of the planetary influences as they affect humanity are neither virtues nor vices; they are qualities common to all who attune themselves to them. They are latent in every human being.

The principle of Mercury is reason; of Venus affection; of Mars energy; of Saturn endurance; of Jupiter preservation; of Uranus constructiveness; and of Neptune mysticism.

The Zodiac holds in solution the various qualities of matter in all its manifold forms. The qualities are indicated by the nature of the signs, and the signs have a definite relation to the constellations. The relationship is, however, not dependent upon the position of the constellations any more than the nature of the radio music is dependent upon the location of the broadcasting station.

The human body possesses innumerable sensory nerves, each of which has an "end organ," whose office is to receive stimuli from without, transmit the vibrations to nerve centers, where in turn they are forwarded by means of the sympathetic system to those organs which are responsive to each particular incoming stimulus, causing chemical changes to take place which give rise to sensation. Sensation produces thoughts in kind. Thoughts determine acts. Acts determine environment.

Before one is conscious of a sensation, a chemical change has taken place, a stimulating vibration has been received which gave the chemical situation an urge and a direction according to the character of the vibration. The vibrations of Mars are positive, exciting, inflammatory; those of Venus are soothing, pacifying, cheering; the vibrations of each planet having its own particular influence.

The influence of Mars is expansive, impulsive, and ever moving. It contains the essence of energy, strength, and motion. It is not an influence to be suppressed, but rather one to be controlled, refined, and directed.

There is not a stone but has a spark of the Martial ray in it, not a planet but feels its animating influence, not an animal that is not moved by its energy, not a human being uncontrolled by its power.

The principle of Venus is love. Love in this sense is not a mere sentimental abstraction; it denotes rather the principle of cohesion operative throughout the universe, the accretive faculty that attracts whatever is in accordance with its nature, whether it be construction or destruction. Nothing is ever lost, for in the Divine Economy creation consists in nothing but recreation—an exchange of the old for the new.

The influence of Jupiter is mainly social, charitable, and religious. Jupiter is the preserving influence of that which manifests as the objective influence of Saturn. Saturn and Jupiter govern the physical conditions, Mars and Venus the emotional nature, and Mercury the mental nature of the human being. The influence of Jupiter is expansive; it favours expression by decoration and adornment, it develops the talent for organization, it influences the unfolding of seeds and buds and creates a fitting environment for the life within them. Jupiter, therefore, brings out all that is sociable, cooperative, and harmonizing.

Every force, whether magnetic, sympathetic, dynamic, or mechanical, is a planetary vibration, and as Jupiter is fourteen hundred times as large as the Earth, the vibrations which he imparts and the force which he exerts is lofty and grand. His influence is for harmony, grandeur, and physical excellence.

Perhaps the most individualistic trait of the Saturnian type is the quality of slowness of inertia. The three qualities inherent in matter are inertia, activity, and mobility. These three qualities are combined in varying proportions in all types of planetary influence, but in the case of Saturn, inertia preponderates.

Those who belong to this type are slow to move, but steadfast and unchanging in action. They are faithful, enduring, unyielding, and fixed. This peculiarity of inertia makes the individual slow to accept new ideas and makes him adhere to old thoughts and methods with great tenacity. One consequence of this type of character is that it keeps what it gets. This is true in terms of ideas, feelings, habits, or actual property. Another consequence is the development of the qualities of concrete exactitude and particularization. Saturn thus favours the expression of the mind through form in sculpture, architecture, and physical science.

There is in Saturn the property of contemplation, which is traced to an innate desire for all arcane wisdom and deep science. This is the secret of Saturn's influence as the Master Builder of character and destiny.

Thus we find Saturn ever willing to accept responsibility, to accentuate it, and to transmute it through the regenerating influence of meditation and contemplation. In a like manner, the influence of Mars is frequently transmuted into devotion, and of Mercury into wisdom.

Saturn thus ever tends to isolation and separativeness; his influence is steadily contractive, ever tending to shape in detail by forming a series of limitations binding the individual to concrete principles.

On the contrary, all that is unlimited and unbound comes under the influence of Uranus.

All metaphysical thought and advanced views find in him a lead; in fact, his influence is so marked and romantic that once it is felt it never can be forgotten.

If the philosopher who draws his influences from Saturn is slow to think, then how much slower is he who draws his influence from Neptune, which is twice as far removed! If one wishes to receive inspiration, he must be very quiet and for a long time. It will be recalled that when Saint John received the Revelation he was put off on the island of Patmos, where he would be undisturbed. He was placed there by his enemies, of course, but they could not have done him a greater good, for here he could let his spirit soar without being molested. It takes time to receive inspiration, but there have been a few men who have been willing to fast forty days in order to be able to reap such reward.

Man is a compound of all the elements. In his early stages, the animal instinct is uppermost and he is conscious only of objects that appeal of his senses. Later, he learns to be conscious of a force within, which appeals to his reason. Finally, he becomes conscious of his unity with the entire universe. He thus passes from the animal to the human, and finally to the divine.

Solar Science is then the spiral stairway that is destined to lead to a glorious future, for instead of simply believing in authority, we can have our faith confirmed by knowledge and our intuition supported by reason.

There comes sometimes into the field of Consciousness a power of spiritual seeking, understanding, and knowing that pales all previous experience within the memory of the particular individual to whom it comes.

These experiences are not common, but are as old as the Human Race; and there is no Sacred Book of Earth's People but that contains allusions to this Rare State of human consciousness—which, eventually, will become the common heritage of an advanced race.

Section Five

Celestial Vibrations

It is the attitude that we assume toward incoming stimuli that suggests and determines the direction and kind of motor discharges or bodily reactions of all kinds. The individual who acts upon impulse is simply following the tendency of the stimulus; hence, he often has occasion to afterwards regret that he has done so.

"The stars incline, but they do not compel." During the spring quarter, nature brings forth new growth, but we may choose not to plant anything and it is easy to predict that with no planting there will be a shortage of food during the following winter.

The wise man does not rule his stars, he rules himself and acts in cooperation with the duly timed operations of nature, the results proving the wisdom of his choice.

On the other hand, we are most apt, under adverse aspects, to feel inharmonious and to act likewise, and thus bring displeasure and opposition, which produce obstacles, limitations, and difficulties.

The word "aspect" is the term that has been adopted to indicate the position of the planets relative to each other and their consequent influence upon the Earth and its inhabitants.

It will readily be seen that if Jupiter gets between Saturn and the Earth, the influence of Saturn is nullified—his vibrations do not reach us. It will thus be seen that the planets are continually forming angles by which they amplify or nullify the effect that might be expected.

An aspect will find response only in those who are attuned to receive that aspect, just as the wireless telegraph receiver is attuned only to the vibration of correspondingly tuned transmitters. Hence, one person may sense the working of an aspect while his own brother may not. The physical process of the effect of an aspect is a change in the chemical constituents of the human body so that some of the fluids are overcome, depleted, or diminished, while others may be increased.

The corresponding change in cell structure draws the attention of the mind to a recognition of disturbance in the body by means of aches, pains, sickness, and weakness.

In the realm of the mind, an adverse aspect of Sun and Saturn tend to mental depression, the extreme effect of which is melancholy, sarcasm, and resentment at apparent restraint and limitations or lack of opportunities. It also inclines to timidity, fear, and a tendency to retrench, quit, back down, and give up the struggle. For it is a struggle to those who are thus affected, and many who are ill succumb because of a preponderance of these feelings, while those who are not strong in a business way feel that the obstacles are too great, and so they fail where stimulating encouragement and kindly assistance from those who understand these aspects would tide them over the period of its influence until normal conditions again prevailed.

The Zodiac has been divided into twelve parts, each division possessing a distinction of its own. It is in these divisions of the Zodiac that the essence radiated by the Sun is incorporated with the gravities characteristic of the particular position of the Zodiac through which they pass, and every physical manifestation in the universe, be it mineral, vegetable, or animal, will express in its nature the character of the particular division of the Zodiac to which it is attuned.

At the moment of birth, when the child draws its first independent breath, filling the lungs and oxygenizing its blood with the elements of the atmosphere which at that moment prevail, according to the nature of the particular planetary aspects operating at that time and place, it receives impressions or tendencies to which it is always afterward responsive whenever like conditions re-occur among the vibratory influences of Zodiacal aspects. People respond to those vibrations or aspects to which they are attuned and they are immune to others.

The sign which is rising at the moment of birth is considered the natural indicator of character, and this will give twelve distinct types, briefly summarized as follows:

Aries. Frank and outspoken, combative, generous, assertive and impulsive, intuitive, yet fond of reason and argument.

Taurus. Dogmatic and obstinate, fearless and strong-willed, patient and determined; affectionate.

Gemini. Dualistic and restless, intellectual and sensational, nervous and irritable; yet kind and generous.

Cancer. Reserved and sensitive, sympathetic and tenacious, impatient yet persistent, impressionable and emotional.

Leo. Firm and self-controlled, persevering and ambitious; faithful, noble, and generous.

Virgo. Retiring and discriminative, yet ingenious; active, thoughtful, and speculative.

Libra. Refined, intuitive, perceptive, ambitious, artistic, sensitive, and just.

Scorpio. Reserved, determined, tenacious, secretive, wise, discreet, firm, proud, and resentful of injuries.

Sagittarius. Active, enterprising, frank, honest, generous, sincere, impressionable, introspective, and demonstrative.

Capricorn. Ambitious, penetrative, receptive, persistent, steady, inspirational, and politically inclined.

Aquarius. Intellectual, retentive, studious, thoughtful, diffusive, versatile, ingenious, and artistic.

Pisces. Emotional, secretive, patient, meditative, kind, generous, imitative, receptive, patient, and peace-loving.

Aries (♈)

Aries is the first sign of the Zodiac. The planet Mars is the ruler of this sign; the mental and martial instincts are here keenly alive, the objective and formative external world being more attractive and fascinating than the subjective, internal, or reflective. It is the first sign of the intellectual trinity.

Those born between March the twenty-first and April the twenty-first are very frank, outspoken, venturesome, self-assertive, ambitious, sensitive, intellectual, enterprising, and entertaining, but are much given to over-estimate, to imagine things to be greater—either better or worse—than they are.

The virtue of this sign may be found in the loyalty of those born under it and in their love of truth and all that is frank, free, independent, generous, and expressive. Mentally, they are very ambitious and always full of enterprise, new schemes, and ideas. They are remarkable for their ability to plan and map out the future, but they rarely develop their own ideas fully themselves.

Taurus (♉)

Taurus is the second sign of the Zodiac. All persons born between April twenty-first and May twenty-first, when the Sun occupies the sign Taurus, are solid, reserved, practical, matter-of-fact, stubborn, determined, patient, plodding, and conservative. They are reliable, honest, and careful in speech and action, and competent to hold positions where dignity and self-reliance are necessary; hence, they usually obtain some government appointment or responsible post in which custom prevails and where authority is well established.

This sign contains the potent energies of the will and the desires, often concealed and suppressed until great provocation releases them, when the pent-up energies of Taurus escape with the force of an explosion.

There is a peculiar psychic side to the practical Taurus nature, which is often developed through the feelings becoming very deeply moved by some exceptional experience. Thought and feeling are very much blended and it is difficult to tell which will be uppermost; for Will and Desire are one in this sign, and those who are morally developed are very intuitive, seeking to control the desire of nature and to purify the emotions.

Mentally, they have great power, but desire is often stronger than the will, and we then find them expressing their mentality in a matter-of-fact manner, as they seem to delight in being what they term "practical." In other words, they are more objective. They possess much concentration and fixity of purpose, but it is difficult to get them to energize their mind, as they seem to love to take things easily and often rely on their intuition more than their reason.

Gemini (♊)

All persons born within the period from May twenty-first to June twentieth will partake more or less of the solar influence expressing itself through the sign Gemini. This is the third sign of the Zodiac and the first of the airy triplicity. It is mutable in quality, signifying duality, like the parts of the body which Gemini governs, such as the lungs, hands, arms, eyes, and ears; being the expresser, or vehicle and medium for carrying out that which is active and latent in the two foregoing signs, Aries and Taurus. This causes all those born under its influence to have the capacity to engage in two pursuits at the same time, giving a love of change and diversity and the special ability to adapt themselves to the requirements of the moment.

The stars Castor and Pollux are so close that they have always been considered twins. They are the most brilliant stars in the celestial sign Gemini. For this reason, Gemini is a dual sign, ruled by the "Twins", and we find that the most frequent trait of character expressed is that of duality.

There are three chief constellations in the celestial sign Gemini.

The first, Auriga, signifies driving power and mechanical ingenuity. The second, Hyades, gives sympathy, which is always associated with a watery sign. The third, Orion, denotes curiosity for research, a disposition to triumph over obstacles, and a love for the beautiful. Thus, the Gemini temperament will be either practical, sympathetic, or artistic, depending upon the particular constellation with which he is in tune.

Another characteristic Gemini complex is the artistic, which expresses as a love of ornament and individuality in drawing and painting. The Pisces sign also produces many artists, but in that sign the talent is developed laboriously, through an innate tendency; while the Gemini artist, more restless and less persistent, and not always so successful, develops because of a love for colour and a desire for expression. The practical tendency of the Gemini also tends to diminish the practice of art, in spite of his artistic disposition and temperament.

Gemini people are more or less inclines toward intellectual pursuits, and are deeply interested in all educational work, and live more in the mind than in the feelings. In fact, they strive all through life to overcome feeling, endeavouring to reason away their sensations. This causes them to be somewhat materialistic, ever hovering between belief and skepticism. They often feel that they want to be in two places at the same time, and are not content to remain in one place for any length of time. Moreover, they seldom finish one thing before commencing another, and this causes them to be somewhat unreliable and indecisive. They have many dual experiences, two courses of action coming prominently into their lives, in respect to which they have to make a choice. They are always more or less nervous, restless, and irritable, which frequently causes them to worry and become diffusive and less concentrated than ever.

When morally developed, they aspire toward a worthy aim, and have the opportunity to live on a plane that is neither wholly objective nor wholly subjective, possessing the ability to see between both modes of manifestation. But when undeveloped morally, mind is everything and then they require to be convinced that there is any state of existence other than the material.

Cancer (♋)

Cancer, which is in power from June twenty-first to July twenty-first, is the fourth sign of the Zodiac, a watery cardinal sign and the first of the maternal trinity. This is the sign in which feeling and emotion are stirred into activity by external means. All persons born when the Sun occupies this sign are sensitive, timid, and retiring, yet tenacious. They are peculiar to themselves, having more noticeable and distinctive characteristics than any other of the signs, the principal being their conventional, yet at the same time attractive, idiosyncrasies. They love to be noticed, but appear to be unassuming and not eager to come forward. They are economical, conservative, retentive, romantic, psychic, and imaginative, and until understood appear to be contrary without the least intention of being so. Cancer persons who are morally undeveloped are mere bundles of moods and inconsistencies, ever wavering and hesitating where feeling and sensation are concerned. But when morally developed, these moods unite in forming a tenacious will or a persistent desire that carries them forward to their goal either by the exercise of tact or by persistent persuasion. They are fond of relics, antiquities and curios, and all things associated with memories of the past.

Leo (♌)

The sign Leo, covering the period from July twenty-first to August twenty-first, is the fifth sign of the Zodiac, fiery, fixed, and royal. All persons born when the Sun was in this sign are powerful, commanding, self-controlled, determined, generous, ambitious, and faithful, having deep emotions. When morally developed, they are attractive and sympathetic; but when undeveloped, they are passionate and hasty, being far too easily led by their feelings.

The main feature of this sign is faith, and those born in it are ever trustful, believing all to be good and pure until found to be otherwise, when they feel most keenly the realization of their misplaced trust.

Leo individuals always aim high, and consequently their ideals are rarely realized. In some cases, they are quite utopian, seeking perfection in all things. They are rarely, if ever, secretive preferring frank and open dealing, even should it entail painful consequences. When much deceived or wronged, they are likely to be proud and contemptuous, but are still magnanimous and forgiving.

The Sun placed in the sign of Leo at birth promises much success in life through personal magnetism and power to adapt oneself to circumstances. The more self-control is developed, the greater will be the success, for then the natural gift of intuition will act freely. Leo people always want to be at the head of things, as they are in possession of good organizing power, being well able to assume authority and command. They rule by a peculiar inner feeling of which they are in possession and which is not common to others, so that in this they in a measure have the advantage over most people. They learn much through the emotional side of their nature, which is powerful and very deep.

Virgo (♍)

The celestial sign Virgo, extending from August twenty-second to September twenty-first, is the sixth sign of the Zodiac, an earthy, mutable sign. All persons born when the Sun is in Virgo are practical, discriminative, critical, methodical, industrious, and intelligent. This is the sign for the business man, the individual who is keenly alive on the physical plane; who does not doubt the existence of the spiritual, but who wastes no time in dreaming or speculating on the unseen, endeavouring to bring all things down to the sensible matter-of-fact everyday world. Those born in this sign are self-possessed, cool, careful, painstaking, cautious, and at the same time active, tactful, alert, and ingenious, with an eye ever open to the "main chance."

There are very few extremes in this sign, these natives being for the most part evenly balanced and cool headed. Virgo people make few pretensions, preferring to work quietly and unobserved. They are not anxious to obtain fame or recognition, but act as discreetly as opportunity will allow.

Those born during the last ten days of August are generally calculating and given to premeditation, rarely, if ever, acting upon impulse. They are retiring and often bashful, and fastidious. Those born from September first to tenth are more thorough. They rise in life through their own merits. They are generally scientific and critical, also sensitive and keenly alive to surrounding conditions. They are competent reasoners, thoughtful and persistent. Those born between the tenth and the twentieth of the month incline more toward a less active life, possessing much more reserve. They are quietly firm.

Libra (♎)

Libra, from September twenty-second to October twenty-second, is the seventh sign of the Zodiac, airy, cardinal, and balancing. It is the first of the Reproductive Trinity. Those born when the Sun is in this sign are very refined and are great lovers of justice. They are sensitive, approbative, fond of pleasure, ambitious, generous, intuitive, harmonious, perceptive, and artistic. All persons born in this sign are well-balanced, amiable, well-disposed, and capable of taking a dispassionate view of life. They see both sides of a subject very clearly. They love to be approved, working well when praised or admired; and they generally merit approval, being pleasant and equable persons to live with. They have excellent perception, never failing to observe clearly all that is going on around them.

There are two extremes born under this influence: Those who are pleasure-lovers, worshippers of form and ceremony, custom, and convention; and those who are very spiritually minded, mentally refined, and keen to appreciate unity in all things.

Those born between September twenty-second and the end of the month are dispassionate, easy-going, very refined, kind, and harmonious. Those born between October first and tenth are lovers of justice, mentally clever, fond of good society, faithful in all their attachments. Those born between October tenth and twenty-second are more material, but keenly intellectual and highly appreciative of mental expression in all forms. They make good partners, as they generally endeavour to preserve harmony.

Scorpio (♏)

The celestial sign Scorpio, October twenty-third to November twenty-first, is the eighth sign of the Zodiac, a fixed and watery sign. All persons born with the Sun in this sign are firm, dignified, controlled, reserved, tenacious, and magnetic. They are tactful, discreet, and cautious. They love approval and appreciate encouragement.

This sign has concealed within it more power than most of the signs. This causes the Scorpio person to be very shrewd and cunning when not morally developed, and to exhibit intense passion and jealousy. Thus, he is likely to be exacting, suspicious, and mistrustful.

Of the three types, those born between October twenty-third and the end of the month are very susceptible to the influence of those around them. They are not talkative, often shy and bashful; but their nature changes considerably on reaching middle age. Those born in the period from November first to tenth, inclusive, are more talkative. They may place too much reliance upon the spoken words of others and suffer in consequence through deception of misplaced confidence. They are hospitable and kind. Those born in the period from November tenth to twentieth are very tenacious, determined, and ambitious. They love public gatherings and society, but are also fond of home and company.

Those born with the Sun in Scorpio are strong characters, and when they overcome pride and jealousy, their power for good in the world is enormous. As they develop, they become more intuitive.

They have strong constitutions, yet have great internal force and recuperative power; they also possess intuitive medical knowledge.

Financially, they succeed by their keen penetration and power to adapt themselves to their environment. They always do well in life, possessing the will power and determination to rise in the world.

Marriage is very important for them, and always beneficial, as they have remarkable powers of attachment, and make excellent parents.

SAGITTARIUS (♐)

Sagittarius, covering the period from November twenty-first to December twentieth, is the ninth sign of the Zodiac, a fiery and mutable sign. All persons born with the Sun in this sign are hopeful, bright, and impressionable, with an instinct for prophecy. They are active, enterprising, loyal, expressive, and given to the demonstration of affection. They are lovers of liberty and believers in freedom of speech; and none know so well how to find the weakest part in another's armour as do Sagittarius people. Nevertheless, they are straightforward, independent, philosophical, and religious in thought and principle.

Of the three types, those born between November twenty-first and the end of the month are very blunt and outspoken and unwilling to submit to any restraint or control. They are fond of science and the practical side of life, taking much interest in details and minute particulars. Those born between December first and tenth are passionate, generous, open and free, fond of argument, high-minded and independent, possessing a love of religious and philosophical studies. Those born between the tenth and the twentieth are more self-willed and at times independent and indifferent, fond of combat and militant in spirit, with a penetrative mind and ready wit.

The mental side of life appeals greatly to the Sagittarian, who is always more or less philosophical, though sympathetic.

The nature of these persons is hopeful and joyous even in advanced years and, although sometimes disturbed, their disposition is generally calm. They are simple in their mode of life and, above all things, delight in independence and will sacrifice everything rather than be under restraint. They fret exceedingly in unsympathetic surroundings. They are watchful and distrustful of others, even of themselves, which sometimes leads to deception whilst trying to avoid it. They love truth, peace, and justice. They are complex and difficult to gauge and fond of theology and spiritual subjects, but inclined to be visionary.

Capricorn (♑)

The celestial sign Capricorn, from December twenty-first to January nineteenth, is the tenth sign of the Zodiac, a cardinal and earthy sign. All persons born when the Sun is in this sign are ambitious and fond of building high ideals of physical splendor and perfection. They are economists, thrifty, persevering, reserved, diplomatic, and profound. They are industrious, painstaking, slow, and cautious, rarely proud or too independent, but having, nevertheless, a fair amount of self-confidence. They are rarely demonstrative or fond of display, and generally are sincere and plain-spoken.

The character of those born under Capricorn is very decided. Their mentality manifests as studiousness, carefulness, thoughtfulness, ability for scientific research, reflection, and meditation.

The health and constitution of those born under the Capricorn influence are affected primarily by the Sun, which is the life-giver. This sign is a retentive sign, and enables those who are born under its influence to cling to physical life as long as it is possible, and they usually live much longer than those born under any other sign, often reaching the age of ninety to a hundred years old and at the same time preserving all the faculties and senses to the end.

All persons fully under its influence are ambitious, careful, thoughtful, prudent, reserved, energetic, persevering, powerful, and enduring.

Aquarius (♒)

The celestial sign Aquarius, January twentieth to February eighteenth, is the eleventh sign of the Zodiac, a fixed airy sign. All persons born with the Sun in this sign are difficult to understand. They are quiet, unobtrusive, patient, faithful, humane, and kind. They love nature, music, art and literature, the intellectual and refined side of life appealing to their humanitarian sense of equality. They are intuitive, honest, and well-meaning, of a studious and thoughtful nature, bent upon fathoming the mysteries of nature.

This sign belongs to the airy triplicity, hence is concerned with the mental region of the Zodiac.

Humanity has not reached that stage when all the qualities that are to be made manifest through the sign Aquarius can be developed. There are very few who completely express the individual characteristics of this sign in our present day, but those who have evolved to where they can express their individual nature are very determined, patient, quiet, and faithful persons. They are philosophical, humanitarian, and exceedingly refined, and they make excellent researchers and scientific writers.

Mentally, they are cautious, steady, intelligent, discriminative, concentrative, studious, and thoughtful, and when they give their minds to study, they can extract more from a subject than any of the other airy signs. There is a tendency for them to live more mentally than physically, and everything belonging to the mental world appeals to them. They usually have a strong healthy constitution, but if they become too concentrative or follow a sedentary life, then there is danger of trouble arising from the defective circulation.

They succeed best as artists, designers, musicians, inventors, electricians, writers, and in any employment where steady, faithful, concentrated work is necessary.

The planet Saturn is their ruler, but it is the metaphysical side of Saturn, which governs the contemplative and meditative qualities. All persons under the Aquarian influence are more or less excellent students of human nature, and their quiet, silent, thoughtful manner always inspires confidence when they are understood by those with whom they come in contact.

Pisces (♓)

The celestial sign Pisces, from February nineteenth to March twentieth, is the last sign of the Zodiac, a mutable, watery sign. All persons born with the Sun in this sign are very receptive, mediumistic, and impressionable. They are not determined nor positive, but persistent, persuasive, and emotional. They are very patient, and do not willingly complain. They are imitative, peaceful, sympathetic, and generous.

In this sign, there are to be found two extremes; but Pisces being a dual sign, these individuals often express both these opposite sides of their character, and hence are not easily understood. They are quite alert and willing to take upon themselves any responsibility if it is to serve a good and useful purpose.

The sign confers upon those under its influence a peculiarly intuitive, receptive condition, which enables them to internally sense and understand things in a totally different way from that of other signs. In character, Pisces people are somewhat over-restless and anxious, and there is a great deal of indecision; but they are able to sense the surrounding conditions, and possess a kind of psychic tendency. The emotions are very strong and are likely to be very much affected by those with whom they come in contact.

Mentally, they are changeable and imaginative, and are always more or less fond of romance, but they possess that peculiar understanding that is not acquired from actual learning, and seem to know things in a strange manner. They are rarely at a loss to explain conditions, and have often been termed "walking encyclopedias." There is one special characteristic that is a distinctive feature of their sign and that is their hospitality and their great love of dumb animals.

Physically, the constitution seems to be easily upset through worry and by being over-anxious and too restless.

All those born in this month appear to be inspirational, and for the most part live in their feelings and emotions. Some of the noblest characters may be found in this sign.

> Get but the truth once uttered and 'tis like a star, new born, that drops into its place, and which, once circling in its placid round, not all the tumult of the earth can shake.

> —**James Russell Lowell**

A Book About You

Section Six

Cosmic Vibrations

Most of us are dead to the wonderful truth outlined in the sky—truths more wonderful, more glorious than any tale of mystery or romance, truths that are continually spread before us in Nature's great book.

The Greeks mapped out the geography of the heavens that is now used more than 1,400 years before Christ. Ptolemy recorded no less than forty-eight of the largest and best known constellations of stars, more than 600 years previous to this, and remember that the telescope was invented only 400 years ago.

Our painted American savages, the Arab in the desert, the simple children on the banks of the Nile, the wild men of the islands of the sea have all been more observant of the mystery hid in the stars than we as a people are today.

The solar system, from the highest spiritual point down to the lowest physical, is one vast organized whole, nowhere dead, nowhere unconscious, nowhere useless, nowhere accidental; but carefully gathered, ordered, and supervised to express the indwelling life and intelligence of its Creator and to subserve His plans. In fact, it is one gigantic Being, throbbing with vitality and consciousness.

The distance of stars from us is so great that it conveys no impression on the mind to state them in miles; some other method, therefore, must be used, and the velocity of light affords us a convenient one. Light travels at the rate of 186,000 miles a second, and by using this as a measuring rod, we can form a better idea of the distance of stars. Thus, the nearest star, Alpha Centauri, is situated at a distance which light requires three and a half years to traverse.

On the average, light requires fifteen and a half years to reach us from a star of the second magnitude, forty-three years from a star of the third, and so on, until, for stars of the twelfth magnitude, the time required is 3,500 years.

How have astronomers ascertained that the star nearest to our solar system is twenty-five trillion miles away? The diameter of the Earth's orbit is 186,000,000 miles; that is to say, that in six months from today, the Earth will be on the other side of the Sun and therefore 186,000,000 miles away from its present position. Now, if we photograph the stars today and six months from now we photograph them again, the second photograph will show that some of the stars have shifted their position ever so slightly with regard to all the rest of the stars. The reason for this shift is easily understood by comparing the stars to a line of lanterns at night. If you stand just a little way off from that line, you will see the lanterns as so many points of light all close together; but if you walk off at right angles for a little distance, you will see them somewhat separated from each other and the nearest ones will appear to be separated from each other more than the farthest ones. This is termed parallax. The Earth in altering its position by 186,000,000 shows us parallax which, for the nearest stars, are great enough for the astronomer to use in calculating their distances. If he can measure the parallax of a star, it is then a slight matter to calculate the distance of that star from the Earth.

The telescope on Mount Wilson, California, is 100 inches in diameter; it took seven years to grind the disk, which is coated with silver. The disk alone weighs four and one-half tons. It does not magnify as is commonly supposed, but simply gathers the light and brings it to a focus. In this case, the reflection is 250,000 times that of the human eye and enables us to penetrate 400 times further into space.

Any magnification may be used in the eye piece, a magnification power of from 3,000 to 6,000 is generally used in viewing the planets. A great clock work motor is used to counteract the apparent motion of the heavens caused by the rotation of the Earth. The movement of this motor is so accurate that a star will remain in the same point in the eye piece as long as may be desired.

The Sun and his family of planets revolve around a central sun, which is millions of miles distant. It requires something less than

26,000 years to make one revolution. His orbit is called the Zodiac, which is divided into twelve signs, familiarly known as Aries, Taurus, Gemini, Cancer, Leo, Virgo, Libra, Scorpio, Sagittarius, Capricorn, Aquarius, and Pisces. It requires our Solar System a little more than 2,100 years to pass through one of these signs, and this time is the measurement of an Age or Dispensation. Because of what astronomers call "the precession of the Equinoxes," the movement of the Sun through the signs of the Zodiac is in order reverse from that given above.

For some years past, the Solar System, which includes our planet Earth, has been entering the Zodiacal sign Aquarius. An airy, mental, electrical sign, which inclines to metaphysical, psychological, progressive, and changed conditions; cooperative and equalizing in its influence. It conduces to investigation, interest in serial matters, means of transit, means of communication, of education, of hygiene, and of new forms of government.

Its planetary ruler is Uranus, called "The Reformer," who destroys but to rebuild better anew. It is Uranus that "makes old things pass away, that all things may become new." It conduces to liberty, freedom, and expression. It has been called the human sign.

The twelve signs are alternately positive and negative in their nature—each contains a certain specialized influence of its own, having a ruler from which the nature of its influence is obtained. The Sun radiates energy to every member of its solar family. As the central figure among the planets, its position indicates the sphere of activity in which the individual will meet with greatest success and is the essential impulse and driving force that urges him to do it.

The Sun is the ruler of all life, the Moon is the giver of all form, and as life manifests through form, the relationship of the Sun and Moon is inseparable, and it becomes the task of every one to subject the Moon or form side of his existence to the Sun or life side, and the degree of success that he attains in doing this will be the measure of his ability to rule his stars.

As the Sun is the Life-giver of the Solar System and the heart is the Life-giver of the Body, it is easy to see why the Sun's influence is the greatest in the nativity of Man, as it operates directly through the heart.

The influence of the Moon is greatest in the first half of life, and the influence of the Sun is the greatest in the second half.

Every planet has definite characteristics that impress themselves upon the child at birth. This is due to the electrostatic condition of the atmosphere at the time of the child's first inspiration of air, by which a vital change takes place in the nature of the blood. For this reason, those who are born under the influence of a particular planet portray the characteristics of that planet most strongly in their mental temperament, and this finds reflection in both motive and action.

In addition to the influence of particular planets, there is the influence of the various constellations. They are usually divided into Cardinal, Fixed, and Mutable signs. The cardinal will make the character acute, active, restless, aspiring, and changeable. The mutable, indifferent, slow, vacillating, and hesitating; yet tractable and impressionable. The fixed will make it determined, decisive, firm, ambitious, and unbending; slow to move, yet irresistible when started.

The constellations easily fall into the following divisions:

Cardinal: Aries–Cancer–Libra–Capricorn

Fixed: Taurus–Leo–Scorpio–Aquarius

Mutable: Gemini–Virgo–Sagittarius–Pisces

The influence of the *cardinal sign* is to stir the latent forces into action, promote change, and create initiative.

The influence of the *fixed sign* is for stability. The individual may be slow and plodding, but he will be persistent; he will know no defeat; he will concentrate upon one point and pursue it to the end; his seal will be almost fanatical.

The influence of the *mutable sign* is flexibility and change. This influence is purely mental or spiritual and gives purpose and incentive to action.

The cardinal type, therefore, is active; the mutable type restless; and the fixed type rigid. As material success depends upon action, the important factors in the world's work are derived from this type.

As stability is a necessary factor in important industrial undertakings, the fixed type frequently share the material and financial success with the cardinal type. The mutable type is, however, adverse to effort—they want adventure, change, travel; they are therefore the promoters who bring manufacturer and inventor together; they are the vendors and middlemen and the agents who negotiate between buyer and seller.

They are also the sensitives, and react more keenly to the experiences of life; they carry the heavier burden because they feel more. They participate in the issues of life to a greater degree because they carry not only their own burden, but the burdens of those around them. The greater possibilities of inner unfoldment, understanding, and development are always with the sensitive. The sensitive uses not only reason, but imagination, vision, intuition, and insight.

The fixed types are usually the materialists who are content with objective possessions and attainments. They use their reason and are interested in that only which can be measured or can be seen, felt, and handled. They are the doers rather than the dreamers and are utterly stable; they fill many responsible positions with great success, and are valuable members of society.

Neither type is superior, they are simply different—both are necessary.

The fixed signs represent something ingathered, collected together, accumulated, and relatively unified; something definite and uniform; a centre of power and possibility, relatively quiescent and unchanging in itself receiving from outside and giving back again when required. They resemble violent explosives, which are inert while they are undisturbed, but contain large stores of energy locked up within them, and produce sudden and violent effects when stimulated to liberate it.

The cardinal signs are always on the surface, never inert, never still, full of activity, ever busy and changing—they attract the most attention in the world.

The mutable signs are intermediate between the two extremes, fluctuate between them, and can ally themselves with either; but they are never so steadfast as the one nor so active and open as the other. In accordance with this, it may be noted that three out of the four mutable signs are described as "double."

In terms of character as applied to the average age man of today, fixed signs indicate persons in whom feeling, desire, or emotion is strong in one or more of the many forms this phase of consciousness can assume. It may be selfish or unselfish according to the impression given their being at the moment of birth by the planetary vibrations prevailing at that time and place.

Such persons are averse to change and have settled views and habits that are very difficult to alter whether good or bad. They vary from the patient and enduring to the obstinate and determined. They sometimes follow one occupation or way of life for a long time without a change. They make faithful friends and unrelenting enemies.

Cardinal signs signify persons who are full of activity, either of body or mind, often of both. They are restless, busy, venturesome, daring, bold, can cut out paths in life for themselves; are innovators, pioneers, abandoning the old and seeking after the new. They are self-reliant and ambitious; often make noticeable, popular, or notorious figures in their sphere of life; may be found occupying public positions, or exercising authority over others. They are generous and impulsive, move and act quickly. They have not the plodding perseverance of the fixed signs, but can work hard and quickly, and achieve much in a short time. They seek rather to mould circumstances to their will than to adapt themselves to circumstances as do natives of mutable signs, or to overcome by dogged persistence as the fixed signs can. They are quick both to love and hate, easily make both friends and enemies, but their feelings may change as quickly. Activity is the keynote of their character, no matter in what channel it may run, whether practical, emotional, or intellectual—and whether for good or evil.

Mutable signs are more difficult to delineate. Adaptability may perhaps express their meaning. In the practical affairs of life, the natives of these signs show neither the activity that moulds circumstances to their will (characteristic of cardinal signs) nor the perseverance and endurance of the fixed signs; but rather seek to gain their ends by adapting themselves to circumstances by intelligent discrimination and the avoidance of extremes. They take the circuitous path when the direct road is not open, and sometimes even when it is open. This tendency shows itself in a great variety of ways. They can adapt themselves to the habits and moods of other people, they can easily see both sides of a question, and can honestly sympathize with quite contradictory opinions and principles. In the sphere of the emotions, this may make them sympathetic, humane, and charitable, and lovers of peace and quietness. Intellectually, it may give a very impartial, subtle, penetrating, and discriminating mind. They are to some extent natural managers, messengers, travellers, or intermediaries, in a general sense; interpret or express the feelings and ideas of others, make writers and speakers of all grades, from clerk to author, from lawyer to preacher.

In the individuality, the cardinal signs give executive ability, and action that is unifying in nature and in accordance with divine law; the mutable signs cognize likenesses, synthesis, and draw together; and the fixed signs give stability and realization of the unity underlying apparent separateness.

These signs may be further differentiated as follows:

Earthy—Practical and material, commercial, intellectual, and scientific.

Watery—Emotional and plastic, sympathetic and resolvent; reproductive.

Airy—Refined and artistic, given to abstract ideas.

Fiery—Spiritual and idealistic, energizing and creative.

They are defined as follows:

Earthy:	Taurus—Virgo—Capricorn
Fiery:	Aries—Leo—Sagittarius
Airy:	Gemini—Libra—Aquarius
Watery:	Cancer—Scorpio—Pisces

Earth is the lowest and outermost of the states of matter; the most differentiated, limited, and complex; and the farthest removed from the state of pure spirit. In its reference to a cosmic plane, it signifies the physical plane; as a state of matter, it means the solid; in reference to man, it means the physical body; as a state of consciousness, it represents action, doing, volition as distinguished from feeling or thinking.

Persons in whose nativity the Earth is predominant show as many modifications and classes as do natives of other elements; but they are generally practical, matter-of-fact people of the world who are better at doing than at thinking or feeling; or who try to reduce thought and emotion to practical applications.

They may be said to be natural executants, but their service varies from that of the prime clerk, the shop assistant, and the laborer; and they range from the wise to the foolish, from the actively ambitious, selfish, or unselfish to the passive, inert, and unenterprising.

Water, as a state of matter, means the liquid state. In its application to a cosmic plane, it signifies the next interior one to the physical, called variously the astral or psychic plane. It expresses consciousness through feelings, emotions, desires, instincts, passions, intuitions; and those who are born under it show both the strength and the weakness of this side of human nature. They vary from the sympathetic, affectionate, charitable, imaginative, sincere, and religious to the indolent, luxury-loving, passionate, selfish, listless, and inert.

Air, as a state of matter, means the gaseous state. It corresponds to sunset and expresses consciousness through thought and understanding. Those who are born under airy signs show many and various gradations of intellect, from the literary to the scientific, from the metaphysical to the poetic, from the busy, practical, and executive to the profound, comprehensive, and solid. The imagination, whether expressed through poetry, music, or art, seems to belong partly to the air and partly to either fire or water.

Fire corresponds to sunrise and to individualization. People coming under fire signs are impulsive, energetic, enthusiastic, positive, impetuous, and active. They seem to resemble the natives of watery signs more than those of earth or air, for they live more in the feelings, emotions, and passions than in the intellect. In so far as it is represented by the Sun, fire may stand for the energizing and all-permeating life of the Universe everywhere, the main-spring of all evolution—all progress.

This, then, is the laboratory in which Nature is forever combining the spiritual forces that result in the infinite diversity on every side, for "All are parts of one stupendous whole."

A Book About You

Section Seven

Light Vibrations

Energy is a mode of motion, and we are conscious of motion by its effect only. This effect, if transmitted to the brain through the vehicle of the eye, makes itself known as light; if it impinges upon the ear, we know it as sound.

Whether this energy shall reach the eye or the ear depends upon the length and frequency of the vibrations.

Radio waves vibrate from 10,000 to 30,000,000 times a second; heat and light waves much faster. Radio waves are therefore extremely long, heat waves shorter, and light waves still shorter.

The length of a wave depends upon its frequency, that is, the number of waves which pass a given point in one second.

We may compare electrical or radio waves to the bass note of a musical scale. As we go up the scale, the waves become shorter and shorter and the frequency higher and higher, until they produce the sensation of heat. If the frequency is increased, visible light waves will appear.

As the frequency is increased, the sensation of light is finally lost; here we contact the ultraviolet or X-ray. As it still further increases, we no longer are conscious of the vibrations, but know them by their effect only.

When the frequency is more than 38,000 vibrations per second, the ear cannot recognize sound; when 400,000,000,000 vibrations have been reached, we perceive the sensation of light, and as the vibrations gradually increase, the eye perceives one colour after another until violet is reached with its 75,000,000,000,000 vibrations a second.

Every phenomenon in nature is what it is by virtue of the rate of motion or vibration.

We speak of the sun as "rising" and "setting," though we know that this is simply an appearance of motion. To our senses the earth is apparently standing still. We speak of a bell as ringing, and yet we know that all that the bell can do is to produce vibrations in the air. When these vibrations come at the rate of sixteen a second, they are then frequent enough to set the tympanic membrane in motion from which the vibration is transmitted along a nerve to the brain, where it is registered as "sound." It is possible for the mind to hear vibrations up to the rate of 38,000 a second. When the number increases beyond this, all is silence again. So we know that the sound is not in the bell, but is in our own mind.

We speak and even think of the sun as "giving light." Yet we know that it is simply giving forth energy that produces vibrations in the ether at the rate of four hundred trillion a second, causing what are termed light waves, so that what is called light is simply a mode of motion, and the only light that there is, is the sensation produced in the mind by the motion of these waves. When the number of vibrations increases, the light changes in colour, each change being caused by shorter and more rapid vibrations; so that although we speak of the rose as being red, the grass as being green, or the sky as being blue, we know that these colours exist only in our minds, and are the sensation experienced by us as the result of a particular rate of vibration. When vibrations are reduced below four hundred trillion a second, they no longer affect us as light, but we experience the sensation of heat.

Scientific observations have shown that the Earth's temperature declines one degree at the height of 100 feet above the Earth's surface, and that there is a difference in temperature corresponding to each 100 feet; and it has been assumed that beyond a certain radius from the Earth's surface—beyond its atmosphere—dense darkness, with corresponding density of cold, reigns supreme.

The French aviator Jean Callizo[1], who holds the world's record and attained a height of 40,820 feet, said that the last observation which he could make of his thermometer showed a temperature of 58 degrees below zero, but soon the mercury sunk out of sight below the armature, so that he had no means of knowing how cold it became. Notwithstanding the fact that he wore four pairs of gloves—paper, silk, wool, and leather—his fingers became numb.

If the Sun gave light and heat as many suppose, all space would be flooded with light; there would be no night because the entire orbit in which the Earth moves would be filled with light. No star would be visible because the stars are not visible in the light.

The Sun is 93,000,000 miles away from the Earth. It is a great dynamo 866,000 miles in diameter. It sends electromagnetic currents throughout all solar space, which is something like six billion miles from end to end. It turns on its axis like the planets, and is but one of thousands of similar systems of suns and planets, many of them much greater in extent, all of them moving forward in space and all revolving around one common center.

It is clear, then, that instead of giving light and heat, the Sun gives forth electrical energy only. This energy contacts with the atmosphere of the Earth in the form of rays. As the Earth is revolving at the incredible speed of more than a thousand miles an hour at its circumference, the atmosphere coming in contact with the electric rays of the Sun becomes incandescent, causing the sensations of light and heat.

As the Earth revolves at a constantly decreasing speed as we reach the poles, the friction becomes less and less and so we find less light and less heat as the poles are reached, until at the poles there is little light and no heat. What we know as light, therefore, appears only in the atmosphere, and not outside of it, and in that part of the atmosphere only which is turned toward the Sun.

---

[1] Pilot Jean Callizo flew from Le Bourget airdome in Paris and flew his plane 12,422 meters. He said, "My eyes felt heavy and I had a consuming desire to sleep...I felt myself puffed out and deformed." This was due to the decrease in atmospheric pressure.

As we ascend from the Earth, the atmosphere becomes more rare, and there is consequently less friction, and therefore less light and less heat.

As the direct rays of electrical energy from the Sun reach only that part of the Earth that is turned toward the Sun, light appears on that side only. The other side of the Earth, being turned away from the Sun, there is no friction and consequently no light, but as the Earth turns upon its axis, the atmosphere gradually comes into direct contact with the electrical rays from the Sun and light appears. The more direct the rays are that strike the Earth, the stronger the friction, the brighter the light, and the greater the heat. This solar phenomenon we call morning, noon, and night.

A man sees because of the activity of the optic nerve, by which light vibrations are communicated to the sensorium, where they produce the images of things. This sensorium is the corresponding center in the brain that is energized by a force connected with the luminiferous ether; hence, the act of seeing is identical with the making of the image of the thing seen. In fact, what we see is the image and not the object.

A reflex is an involuntary act. When light, which is radiant energy, strikes the eye, the pupils contract. These animal reflexes exceed in sensitivity any apparatus yet devised by man.

The retina of the eye is 3,000 times more sensitive than a photographic plate. The sense of smell surpasses in fineness the most impressionable scientific instruments. The lungs antedate the bellows; the heart, the pump; the hand, the lever; and the eye, the photographic camera.

Telephonic and telegraphic apparatus duplicate mimetically what has always been done by the nervous system and always by aid of the same energy.

Scientists make use of the word "ether" in speaking of the substance "in which we live and move and have our being;" which is omnipresent, which interpenetrates everything, and which is the source of all activity. They use the word "ether" because ether implies something which can be measured, and so far as the materialistic school of science is concerned anything that cannot be measured does not exist. But who can measure an electron?[1] And yet the electron is the basis for all material existence, so far as we know at present.

A number of electrons equal to twenty-five million times the population of the Earth must be present in the test tube for a chemist to detect them in a chemical trace. About 125 septillions of atoms are in a cubic inch of lead. And we cannot come anywhere near even seeing an atom through a microscope.

Yet the atom is as large as our solar system compared to the electrons of which it is composed.

All atoms are alike in having one positive central sun of energy around which one or more negative charges revolve.

The diameter of an electron is to the diameter of the atom as the diameter of our Earth is to is to the diameter of the orbit in which it moves around the sun. More specifically, it has been determined that an electron is one-eighteen-thousandth of the mass of a hydrogen atom.

It is clear, therefore, that matter is capable of a degree of refinement almost beyond the power of the human mind to conceive. We have not as yet been able to analyze this refinement beyond the electron, and even in getting thus far have had to supplement our physical observation of effect with imagination to cover certain gaps.

From all this, it is plain that the electron is merely an invisible mode of motion—a charge of electrical energy.

Light is then a mode of motion. For it results from the oscillation of the infinitesimal particles that impinge on the cells and awaken the transmuted motion that we call seeing.

---

1 We can. The mass of an electron has been measured as 9.11×10^{-31}kg. The "classical electron radius" has been measured at 2.8179×10^{-15}m. The classical radius is a tad outdated, since it does not take into account quantum charge, but it is still useful in certain calculations.

The solar fluid is also the medium for the transmission of the potencies organized by the various planets. It holds in solution the basic elements of life. It is the only possible fluid that is sufficiently subtle to carry the delicate vibrations that are constantly being broadcasted over the radio, and which penetrate iron, steel, and every other barrier, and which are not limited by either time or space.

The movement of the planets cause vibrations in the ether. The nature of the vibrations which they send depend upon the particular nature of that planet, as well as its ever changing position in the Zodiac. These emanations are constantly being impressed upon all the worlds of our system by the perfect conductivity of the solar ether.

Throughout the entire Universe, the law of cause and effect is ever at work. This law is supreme; here a cause, there an effect. They can never operate independently. One is supplementary to the other. Nature at all times is endeavouring to establish a perfect equilibrium. This is the law of the Universe and is ever active. Universal harmony is the goal for which all nature strives. The entire cosmos moves under this law. The sun, the moon, the stars are all held in their respective positions because of harmony. They travel their orbits, they appear at certain times in certain places, and because of the precision of this law, astronomers are able to tell us where various stars will appear in a thousand years. The scientist bases his entire hypothesis on this law of cause and effect. Nowhere is it held in dispute except in the domain of man. Here we find people speaking of luck, chance, accident, and mishap; but is any one of these possible? Is the Universe a unit? If so, and there is law and order in one part, it must extend throughout all parts. This is a scientific deduction.

Ether fills all interplanetary space. This more or less metaphysical substance is the elementary basis of all life and matter.

Matter in motion represents kinetic energy. Ether under strain represents potential energy, and all of the activities of the material universe consist of alterations from one of these forms of energy to the other.

The movement of the planets represents kinetic energy, matter in motion. For instance, Uranus is a mass of matter more than one hundred thousand miles in circumference. This tremendous amount of material substance is driving through the ether at the rate of four miles a second, as it has a diameter of 34,800 miles it puts at least 34,800 miles of ether under strain, driving it forward with a velocity of four miles a second, and what is of still more importance, the planet is not only moving forward, but is revolving upon its axis. It will then not only push the ether forward, but will twist it into spiral form. These spiral vibrations are potential energy.

Uranus enters the sign of Aries in the spring of 1927. Aries is a cardinal, fiery sign. Those who come under the influence of this sign are ambitious, versatile, enterprising, forceful, determined, headstrong, impulsive, fiery, and quick tempered.

Mars is the normal ruler of the sign and brings enterprise, daring, energy, and progress.

But the vibrations from Uranus create an abnormal situation: Enterprise will be converted into strife, daring into friction, energy into accident, ambition into enmity, construction into destruction. The powerful electrical vibrations from Uranus, contacting the fiery vibrations of Aries, will have a tendency to break down existing conditions, and in doing so bring about fractures, dislocations, sudden catastrophes, alienations, ruptures, and separations.[1]

All that is unlimited and unbound comes under the influence of Uranus. His mission is to awaken and revivify, remodel, and renew the life of those who come under his magic spell.

Swift and unexpected, he brings thunderbolt catastrophes and experiences unthought of, for with him indeed it is "the unexpected that always happens."

He waits to afflict, but out of his evil always comes good. He gives no warning as to the nature of his lightening-like cataclysms, but

---

[1] It should be noted that the world was plunged in the Great Depression in 1929; Adolf Hitler came to power in 1934; and World War II raged in 1939.

comes laden as it were, with a mixture of colours, the hues of which are peculiarly interwoven with the colour of the vibrations with which he meets.

We may then expect to find a great conflict of natural forces during the next few years—storms, disasters, unseasonable weather—with consequent destruction of life and property. These are the natural and inevitable results of the conflict of unseen forces, and there seems to be no way of evading or avoiding the result of this invisible warfare.

But unfortunately, the result does not stop here. The vibrations reach the minds of men and act upon the impulses and emotions, and unless the affairs of the nation are in the hands of men who recognize the danger and know how to modify, adjust, or control the situation, the result is war.

War is simply the result of ignorance and prejudice. Try to visualize the result of this lack of knowledge concerning natural laws. Can you realize the situation? Think for a moment. See the army of the dead pass in review, the greatest army ever gathered together in the history of the world. Men from Germany, from France, from Italy, from England, from Belgium, from Austria, from Russia, from Poland, from Rumania, from Bulgaria, from Serbia, from Turkey, yes and from China, Japan, India, New Zealand, Australia, Egypt, and America—on they go, silently, noiselessly, for the dead are very quiet, marching all day long and all the next day, and the day after still they come. Day after day, week after week, and month after month, for it would take months for this army of ten million men to pass any given point. All dead and dead only because a few men in high places did not know that force can always be met with equal or superior force; they did not know that a higher law always controls a lower law, and because intelligent men and women allowed a few men to control their thinking processes, the entire world must sit in sackcloth and ashes, for the living will find it necessary to work the rest of their lives in order to even pay the interest on the obligations assumed during the last war, and their children will find these obligations an inheritance, which they in turn will pass on to their children and their children's children.

"Though the mills of God grind slowly,
Yet they grind exceedingly small,
Though with patience He stands waiting,
With Exactness grinds He all."

—Henry Wadsworth Longfellow

Section Eight

Sound Vibrations

All that the ear perceives in the beautiful and wonderful music of a symphony orchestra is simply motion of one dimension, or motion in a straight line.

Noise and tone are then simply terms of contrast. Noise is due to a non-periodic vibration. Tones are sounds having continuity and containing such characteristics as pitch, frequency, intensity, and quality.

The vibrations produce various effects in the atmosphere, such as displacements, velocities, and accelerations, as well as changes of density, pressure, and temperature.

Because of the elasticity of the atmosphere, these displacements occur periodically and are transmitted from their source in radial directions. These disturbances as they exist in the air constitute sound waves.

Nearly all methods for recording sound waves make use of a diaphragm as the receiver.

The ear drum, the telephone receiver, the phonograph, and the radio illustrate the method by which the diaphragm is set in vibration by the direct action of sound waves.

A diaphragm responds with remarkable facility to a great variety of tone combinations; the telephone and radio are convincing evidence of the degree of perfection attained by these instruments.

But what is still more wonderful is the fact that a diaphragm in reverse action may set up vibrations and thus reproduce sound waves of any description, as is done by the diaphragm of the phonograph, which is mechanically pushed along by the record.

The intensity of a simple vibratory motion varies as the square of the amplitude. For this reason, vibrations in their original form are usually inaudible because they do not cause waves in the atmosphere, as illustrated by the string of a violin without the instrument, or the reed of the clarinet without the tube.

A sound producing instrument has two functions—the generator and the resonator—which may be illustrated by the strings of a piano and the sound board; the vocal cords of the human body and the mouth; the diaphragm of a drum and the body; the mouth of an organ and the tubes.

It will readily be seen that the resonator can give no tones except those received from the generator. The quality of the tone will then depend upon the degree of sympathy which exists between the generator and the resonator.

To tune, a sounding body is then to adjust the resonator to its natural period of specified frequency. When they are in tune, the response will be of the maximum efficiency; but when they are out of tune, there will be little or no resonance, and consequently no efficiency.

Hearing is the sensation produced by the auditory nerve: Sound vibrations are communicated to the brain and thence within the consciousness. The auditory nerve communicates the vibrations of the sonoriferous ether in such a manner as to duplicate the sound vibrations within. Hence, it is the action of this energy energizing the nerve that produces the sensation of hearing, which is in reality the reproduction within us of that which is heard.

To make this clear, there may be a beautiful love song, a military march, or a funeral dirge in the air, but you are conscious of neither without the use of an amplifier; but with the use of this instrument, you may listen to either of these by a simple selective process, and your emotion of love, or of triumph, or of sorrow is aroused by the different vibrations that have been projected into the ether from a broadcasting station thousands of miles away.

The energy coming from the Sun during the day interferes with sound. For this reason, radio is always more efficient after sundown, and in winter rather than summer. In other words, audibility is increased as light decreases.

During the total eclipse of the Sun that took place September 10, 1923, the efficiency of the radio increased more than fifteen times while the eclipse was taking place. To be exact, the audibility of the radio at nine o'clock in the morning of the day of the eclipse was 32, while at the maximum or totality it was 490.

The ether is the universal connecting medium that binds the universe together and makes it a coherent whole instead of a chaotic collection of independent isolated fragments. It is the vehicle for the transmission of all manner of force.

It is therefore the storehouse of potential energy. It is the one all-permeating substance that binds the whole of the particles of matter together. It is the uniting and binding medium without which, if matter could exist at all, it could exist only as chaotic and isolated fragments.

It is the universal medium of communication.

The activities of nature are reduced to a series of laws through the discovery of underlying causes, and these causes are found through the observation and classifications of correspondences.

There are no new laws. All laws are eternal—they never change. They have always been in existence and will always continue to be in existence. All manifestations of physical life depend upon these laws. The laws governing chemical combinations, the conservation of energy, electric radiation, chemistry, and physics are all applicable in the organic domain, and the conditions and experience with which we meet depend upon our understanding and application of these laws.

The great advantage that the violin has over all other orchestral instruments is due to the control the performer has over the instrument. This tone quality, as well as the wave form, remains constant so long as the bowing is constant in pressure, speed, and direction.

These wave forms arouse emotion of gaiety, passion, force, gloom, or anger by causing vibrations in the nerves of the sympathetic system. *with a ⬤ violin! OR guitar*

The emotions are the gateways of the soul, the most holy place. All sciences lead to the threshold of this unseen vestibule and point within.

Music is the science of sound, tones, rhymes, mathematical ratios, and even silences, all conveyed by mere vibrations in the ether which are the only means of action; and yet with these, the deepest and most profound emotions are aroused. One whose heart is hopelessly callous to the spoken message and impervious to the written word can be reached by the invisible, impalpable, incomprehensible, unspeakable pathos aroused by the ethereal vibrations of the trained musical artist.

But, however great the artist, his place in the scheme of things will depend upon his ability to act in harmony with his environment. For if each member of an orchestra were to play regardless of his fellow players, the combined result would be a painful discord, although separately each might produce an agreeable harmony.

We are each an integral part of an organic whole, and must therefore act in concert. Each must be consciously attuned to the others and perform his particular part as related to the whole. He must not interfere with the parts of others, nor play a solo when a symphony is the program.

The golden tone of the cornet, the bird-like warble of the flute, the stately sonority of the trombone, the reedy richness of the clarinet, the ringing clarity of the bell, the brassy note of the bugle, the dulcet blending of the violin, the enchanting sweetness of the harp, the enticing notes of the piccolo, and the martial roll of the drum are all necessary and essential in the grand ensemble of the orchestra.

The instant a piece of music is broadcasted, by putting the proper mechanism to your ear, you can get it as clearly and distinctly as though you were in the same room. This indicates that these vibrations proceed in every direction. Wherever there is an ear to hear, it may hear.

If, then, there is a substance so refined that it will send the sound of a musical instrument in every direction so that every human being who is equipped with the proper mechanism may receive the message, is it not possible that the same substance will carry a thought just as readily and just as certainly?

If it is possible to arouse the emotion of love or power or fear by sending vibrations through the ether for thousands of miles in such a manner that anyone may contact them, is it not also possible that any emotion, any thought, may be sent in the same manner, provided only that the sending station be sufficiently powerful?

It is, but these thoughts, emotions, and feelings are not received consciously, for the very excellent and simple reason that we are conscious of nothing except that which reaches us through one of the five senses.

The five senses are the only method by which we may contact the objective world, and as we can not see a thought, nor can we hear it, taste it, smell it, or feel it, there is no way by which we can become conscious of it.

But that does not mean that we do not get it, in fact by far the largest proportion of our thought reaches us subconsciously or intuitively.

The subconscious is provided with an entire system of nerves reaching every part of the body, and this system is entirely separate and distinct from the objective, it is called the sympathetic. Every pore of your skin is provided with a tiny hair which is an antennae reaching out into space and is infinitely more sensitive than the antennae that receives the messages on you radio. This is why and how the wild animals of the jungle receive messages of danger long before the hunter ever sees them. They sense the danger and are off.

Thought is the vibratory force caused by the action of the brain upon the mental ether. When we think, the mind must first be energized by a particular energy. This energizing of the mind causes it to act upon the stimulus of that energy, and a thought is made in the mind as a result of such energizing. There is then the energizing of the brain, the mental action of thinking, and the making of the thought as a result of such thinking. Begin to think. The thoughts will follow each other in rapid succession. One thought will suggest another. You will soon be surprised at some of the thoughts which have made you a channel of their expression. You did not know that you knew so much about the subject.

You did not know that you could put them into such beautiful language. You marvel at the ease and rapidity with which the thoughts arrive. Whence do they come? From the One Source of all wisdom, all power, and all understanding. You have been to the source of all knowledge. Every thought that has ever been thought is still in existence, ready and waiting for someone to attach the mechanism by which it can find expression. That mechanism is the brain. You can therefore think the thoughts of every sage, every artist, every financier, every captain of industry who has ever existed, for thoughts never die.

Back of the beating hammer,
By which the steel is wrought,
Back of the work-shops clamor,
The seeker may find the thought;
The thought that is ever master
Of Iron and Steam and Steel,
That rises above disaster,
And tramples it under heel!

–Burton Bradley

Section Nine

Color Vibrations

The varying velocities of light contain all the splendors of the universe. The velocities decrease from white light (186,000 miles a second) through violet, indigo, blue, green, yellow, orange, and red to black (140,000 miles a second). It is by the varying movements of theses velocities that the eye is affected by the sensation known as color.

The molecular constitution of a body determines the character and speed of the light vibrations it returns to the eye, and thus gives each body its own characteristic color. Hence, the term "color" is used to denote the different appearances that matter presents to the eye independent of its form.

Black is composed of equal parts of red, yellow, and blue. White is composed of five parts of red, three parts of yellow, and eight parts of blue. Normal or natural gray is composed of white and black in equal proportions. Black, therefore, means the result of all colors, while white signifies the reflection of all colors; and each color in its turn is but a mode of motion, or the varying sensations that we experience when these vibrations impinge upon the optic nerve.

Color is, therefore, one of the manifestations of vibration and all vibration manifests in corresponding color, the color being merely an indication of the occult chemical activity.

The color indicates not only the quality but the value of any chemical substance by reason of its own particular rate of vibration, and all objects of any particular color have that vibratory activity and vibratory value which pertain to that color. As the color is, so is the vibration.

Nature's scale of vibration is very wide in its extent. It commences with sound, then merges into thermal heat waves, and these vibrations climb the vibratory scale as the temperature increases and merge into the vibrations of the radiant heat waves in the infrared which reach up to the visible red of the light spectrum.

The vibrations above the infrared are:

Visible Red	15 trillions
Orange	20 trillions
Yellow	28 trillions
Green	35 trillions
Blue	50 trillions
Indigo	60 trillions
Violet	75 trillions

The sensation of color, therefore, depends on the number of vibrations of light ether, just as the pitch of a note depends on the number of vibrations of the sounding body. The number of vibrations for each color is constant. These seven different rates of vibration that we know as colors make up the visible light spectrum. Beyond these are series of vibrations known as the ultra-violet. These extend up to those vibrations designated as radioactivity, of which radium and the X-rays are best known examples. This ends both the light spectrum and nature's vibratory scales so far as present knowledge goes. As the quality and value of all forms of energy are due to their rates of vibration, it follows that color will indicate the quality of the vibrating energy.

Color, like the diatonic scale, is divided into seven distinct notes.

Red has a stimulating effect. The disturbing influence of red is well illustrated by the expression "painting the town red," indicating recklessness and destruction.

Yellow is a nerve tonic. It is the climax of luminosity, and symbolizes sunlight itself. It produces the feeling of joy and gaiety.

Green has a quieting and soothing effect. It is the color of nature and suggests life. It checks mental activity and suggests sleep.

Blue suggests space, vastness. It is depressing and chilling. One who is continually in a blue environment will sooner or later have the "blues." It is a melancholy color.

Violet is magnetic and cooling.

Each color has a distinct frequency or vibration due to wave lengths. Red has a larger wave length than blue, which is proportionately much shorter. That is why the quick notes of the drums arouse the emotions of the savage—they express in sound what red expresses in color, while the neutral notes of the flute or horn have a quieting influence. They express in sound what blue expresses in color.

These manifestations are recognized as they are perceived by the different nerves, for the mind of man translates the impressions of the world into facts of consciousness and thought by means of the nerves. All these varying rates of vibration differ only in direction, rate, and frequency, and are interpreted according to the different nerves or groups of nerves physically attuned to them or organized to select and respond to especial manifestations of vibratory activity.

Color is both physical and psychological in its effect upon the mind. The physical effect is a chemical one; the psychological effect is psychic. The nervous system reflects its disturbances upon the mind; hence the sensation of pain or pleasure and the emotional states that accompany them. This is true of all the colors. Primary colors are radical, elemental, and fixed in their vibrations or wave lengths, and hence, when once the effects of the sensations which they produce on the mind are known, their uniformity can always be depended upon.

Red is thermal and a stimulant and blue is electrical and depressing. They act uniformly on all forms of life. The spectrum analysis proves that the seven colors of light are made up of vibrations or wave lengths of mathematical exactness.

As all vibratory activity expresses itself in form, color, and sound, it follows that the energy is always of that particular color, shade, or tint that belongs to that particular rate of vibration. This is true not only of those colors, shades, and tints that are perceptible to visible light, but also of the finer forces of nature that transcend the physical senses.

All energy of whatever quality is continually vibrating and, by reason of this vibration, it assumes the color, shade, or tint belonging to that specific rate of vibration.

The primary colors are red, blue, and yellow. All the other colors are combinations of these colors in certain proportions. Red is the physical color and is the color of all physical energy. The various shades of red have their various significations, but, generally speaking, red is the physical color.

Red is also the color of the will. Where ever the will is expressed, it assumes the red color because Will is the out-flowing or manifesting principle, the extension or expression of the self into manifestation. Therefore it must express itself in and through the physical; consequently, it becomes red in color.

The second primary color is blue, the color of emotion. All energy vibrating on the higher octave is either blue or red according as it is positive or negative—blue being the negative, feminine, or magnetic side of matter and red the positive, masculine, or radiant side. The bluer the matter may be, the more magnetic it is, while the redder it may be the more electrical it is. Will and Desire are thus the two poles of etheric matter—Will being red, Desire being blue.

The third primary color is yellow and it is the color of the mental plane. Everything vibrating on the mental octave is yellow. The darker the yellow, the more gross and material is the character of the thought; the lighter it becomes, the more spiritual it is. The clearer the yellow is, the more purity of thought. The brighter the yellow, the more brilliancy of mind is indicated.

Yellow or orange symbolize the highest function and power of our nature and preeminently typify the "scientific" temperament.

White is really the combination of all the seven colors. They are all found to unite in forming the white ray. The prism has the power of breaking up the white light into seven prismatic rays, therefore white light is really the combination of those rays.

Pure white is unity. It is in fact the very essence of balance. It is the star of hope that typifies cleanliness and symbolizes power. It is the language of knowledge, expression, and spirituality.

Virgin white not only signifies cleanliness, but purity; and naturally, the mind is consciously as well as unconsciously affected by it.

Black is the reverse of white. White indicates the spirit. Clack indicates extreme materiality; not materiality in the sense of physical substance, but materiality as the antithesis of spirit. Black indicates the disintegration which leads to annihilation.

Black is repressing, depressing, and suppressing. It represents the negative conditions of gloom, fear, error, disease, ignorance, pessimism, and hopelessness.

Black typifies the universal negative in which all color is hid, absorbed, and is emblematic of death, oblivion, and annihilation.

Scarlet is the color of anger, the color which the astral body assumes when it is in an intensely angry condition. Anger is really the forcible action of the will moving outward in a very positive manner. This is what produces the state of anger.

The color of ether is pink, although its vibration is so intense that very few are able to see the vibration; but ether is always pink. Crimson is the color of affection and human feeling. It is the self-relative color, because our affection is given to persons on account of their particular relation to us.

Affection is purely a physical and animal feeling.

Rose is the color of life, and as we approach the physical it is more red. As life is brought under the influence of the emotions, it takes on whatever color is found, blended with this red or rose color.

Indigo blue is the color of occultism. The dark indigo partakes of the element of sorcery, while the pure indigo is emblematic of pure occultism.

Violet is the color of magic because it is so far above the ordinary rate of vibration that it has the power of neutralizing and even transforming those rates into its own, thus giving the power of alchemy.

Purple being blue mixed with red, the positive aspect of emotion, is the color of mastership, and indicates the master.

Lavender, which is a great deal of white mixed with purple, indicates the master on the astral plane, but merging toward the spiritual.

Green is the color of action. It is expressed by minor chords, and is the positive expression of the inner being as expressed through action.

Unselfish action—action which is purely altruistic in its character, which has no relation whatever to the individual—is a clear emerald green, and the nearer this approaches to the spiritual the paler it becomes.

Brown is, in a sense, a mystical color, in that it indicates the presence of white, red, and black in certain combinations. As the shade is, so will its influence be.

As all the colors are included in the white, so is all matter built up of simpler or elementary substances and all changes are due to distribution and aggregation of the elementary matter.

Motion is the primary cause that gives rise to color and all other phenomena in existence.

In order to trace the origin and progress of any effect, visible or invisible, the aim must be to determine the movement or movements which brought the phenomena into existence.

The principle of vibration permeates the whole science of radiation or motion and may be stated in a general way by saying that a body absorbs waves that are of the same period as those which it emits when it is itself in vibration.

The essential condition is therefore that the receiver shall be in the same key or wave length as the sender or origin of the movement.

The original wave gives energy to the wave upon which it impinges. While one is gaining energy, the other is losing it and this continues until the process of absorption is completed.

This principle applies to light, heat, sound, color, or energy of any kind, where it is distributed by a process of radiation.

> Silently sat the artist alone,
> Carving a Christ from the ivory bone.
> Little by little with toil and pain,
> He won his way through the sightless grain
> That held and yet hid the thing he sought,
> Till the work stood up, a growing thought.
>
> **—Boker's "Ivory Carver"**

A Book About You

Section Ten

Heat Vibrations

The influence of heat is so beneficent and sometimes so terrible that it is not surprising that from time immemorial it should have received not only the attention but sometimes the adoration of mankind.

It is through the agency of heat that all animal and vegetable life comes into being. Without heat there could be no life as we know it upon the planet.

Heat is the sensation produced by the motion of atoms of matter. If we pass the various effects of heat in review, we shall find that matter and motion are the necessary correlations of heat.

Heat coming in contact with certain substances brings about the phenomena that we call combustion. This is caused by the union of oxygen and carbon, which union produces at once both heat and light. The result is the disintegration of the substance.

There are other causes of combustion that proceed more rapidly. Take for instance a piece of gun-cotton. Gun-cotton is a combination of hydrogen, oxygen, and nitrogen. When heat is applied, the four kinds of atoms will become immediately disassociated leaving no trace of the gun-cotton. Where did it go? The carbon and a part of the oxygen formed carbonic gas, the rest of the oxygen combined with the hydrogen and formed vapor. The nitrogen remained free.

It will then be seen that heat does not change the nature of the atoms, it simply changes their respective positions with regard to each other.

The application of heat not only brings about a chemical change in the nature of the substances, but in so doing it liberates energy, and what is most interesting to observe the energy that is liberated is always solar energy.

In the combustion of coal, it is the remains of immense forests that existed upon the earth long before the advent of man. These forests depended for their existence upon the energy that they received from the Sun. We now burn the coal, which liberates the energy that was radiated by the Sun to the earth thousands of years ago and has been preserved intact.

If we apply the heat to water, we are simply combining the solar energy stored up in the wood or coal with the water and thereby converting it into vapor.

If we make use of hydraulic power, we are again utilizing the energy of the Sun that was required to lift water from ocean or lake and carry it to the mountain top.

The energy of the wind is but the force that is transmitted to the atmosphere by the condensation of vapor and is therefore received from the Sun.

All animal life is dependent upon food and this food is but the result of the action of solar energy upon the earth. Each atom of hydrogen in the blood of an animal disengages a certain specified amount of solar energy, and this in turn combines with oxygen and makes restitution to nature in another form.

Lines of energy crossing a center never fail to intensify at the focus into heat or light or both. Suspended energy passing the intensified local centers becomes fixed in a state of rest, and materializes into static matter.

Matter is the sleep state becomes the core of the resistance to energized influx and the suns come into being, the focal centers and arc lights of the deep.

There is a bridge between energy and matter that is invariably used. That bridge is heat, which expresses according to the energy applied, resistance met and time consumed. If it be a great resistance and confined to a short time, the heat will be intense; if it be a lesser resistance or a longer period of time consumed, the heat will in like ration be reduced or extended. Not because there is a less quantity of heat, but because it is extended in keeping with the greater or lesser time used.

Matter in motion and ether under strain constitute the fundamental concrete things we have to deal with in physics. The first represents kinetic energy, the second potential energy; and all the activities of the material universe are produced by alterations from one of these forms to the other.

Energy is a potential force in the state of action, while matter is expended energy in the state of rest. Energy is prior to matter, a finer composition and more susceptible to the influence of Natural Law. Out from the eternal principles of nature, slowly the endless sea of cosmic energy came into being. The eternal silence was the womb that gave birth to the ocean of life.

Whenever the transference and transformation of energy occur, some effect is produced; but the energy is never diminished in quantity. It is merely passed on from one body to another.

Energy depends upon the rate of motion—that is the mass multiplied by the velocity—and we therefore find the greatest quantities of energy passing through stellar space, for certainly the heavenly bodies contain the greatest mass and attain the highest velocity. It has been calculated that the sun is distributing energy into space at the rate of 12,000 horsepower per square foot of surface.

The ether, then, is the great vehicle of energy and the medium in which all energy originates. This energy passes from potential to kinetic and back again. For example, when a planet is at the farthest point form the sun, her velocity will be least; consequently, her kinetic energy is least. As she rounds the farthest point in her orbit and begins to approach the sun, she acquires kinetic energy at the expense of potential energy. When nearest the sun, her velocity is greatest and her potential energy is least. As she rounds the nearest point and begins to retreat, her kinetic energy begins to diminish; it is used up in combating the powerful attraction of the sun.

Such is the ebb and flow throughout all nature of the visible energies of the universe, and herein will be found an explanation for the different effects produced upon mankind by the planets as they continually change their location—all changes and phenomena being due to variations of the ethereal waves caused by the movement of stellar bodies, or mass multiplied by velocity.

The sun contains enormous quantities of helium. Helium comes from radium and radium is a storehouse of the most concentrated energy known to man. It is a source of energy that will liberate three or four million times as much heat as any chemical reaction known, and continue to do this in almost unlimited quantity.

The molecule is a structure formed by a combination of carbon, nitrogen, oxygen, and hydrogen; the four atoms which represent earth, air, fire, and water. These four elementary atoms form the various molecules from which eighty-six chemical elements are composed.

The character of the elements depends upon the proportion in which the four elementary atoms are united, each element contributing its rate of vibration in accordance with the proportion in which it is present in the combination.

These eighty-six different chemical elements constitute the basis for every group of matter, organic or inorganic, and the only difference in the elements is in the rate of vibration or the vibratory activity of the molecules of which the structure is composed.

The constitution of matter is therefore simply a mode of motion, all form being the result of the vibratory motion of the cosmic energy.

The material changes that take place are caused by changes in atomic structure, and the changes in atomic structure are in turn the result of alterations in the vibratory motion of the cosmic energy. Because of these facts, we see that transmutation is not only entirely possible, but must actually take place continually.

The different manifestations of energy are: gravitation, heat, light, electricity, magnetism, chemical affinity, cohesion, and adhesion or molecular attraction.

The law of gravitation is: Every substance in the universe attracts every other substance with a force jointly proportional to the mass of the attracting and of the attracted body, and varying inversely as the square of the distance.[1]

Light, heat, magnetism, electricity, chemical affinity are only different modes of one and the same energy, and each can, directly or indirectly, be converted into the original form from which it was taken.

Cosmic power, whether static or dynamic, can neither be increased nor lessened. But since scientists will accept for truth only that which can be demonstrated by experiment or by calculation, and since it is far more difficult to measure and calculate forces than to weigh matter, the rotation of force remained a mystery for many years; and not until recently has this theorem been recognized and demonstrated. It is now, however, secured and uncontested recognition.

To react chemically, two bodies must contain intrinsic energy at different chemical potentials. When such bodies are brought together, a part of the intrinsic energy of one or both is transferred into such new forms of combination as are stable under the new conditions.

We use the word "adhesion" to denote the attractions exerted between particles of two different bodies when placed in contact with one another. On the other hand, when particles of different bodies have such an attraction for each other as to rush together and form a substance of a different chemical nature, then we have the operation of chemical affinity.

When a substance is heated, it gives out part of its heat to a medium that surrounds it. This heat-energy is propagated as undulations in the medium, and proceeds outward with the enormous velocity of 186,000 miles per second. If the temperature of the hot substance be not very great, these undulations do not effect the eye, but are invisible, forming rays of dark heat; but as the temperature rises, we

---

1 This is Newton's Law of Universal Gravitation which he formulated and forst published in his book *Principia Mathematica* in 1687.

begin to see a few red rays, and we say that the body is "red hot." As the temperature still continues to rise, the body passes to a yellow and then to a white heat, until it ultimately glows with a splendour like that of the Sun.

This splendour of the Sun is but an indication of the nature of the process that is taking place, for light, heat, and energy are but the process of releasing solar energy.

Through the process of combustion, the vanished sunshine that has been laid up in wood or coal is again liberated.

The force that urges forward the locomotive is simply sunshine converted into power.

In 1857, Mr. Murray of London published a biography of the famous English engineer, George Stephenson[1], in which an interesting description of the light and heat cycle is given:

On Sunday, just when the company had returned from church and were standing on the terrace overlooking the railway station, a train rushed by, leaving a long line of white steam behind.

"Now," said Stephenson to Buckland, the well-known geologist, "can you tell me what power moves that train?"

"Why," replied the other, "I suppose it is one of your big engines."

"But what moves the engine?"

"Oh, probably one of your stout Newcastle engine-drivers."

"What do you say to the light of the sun?"

"What do you mean?"

"Nothing else moves the engine," said the great engineer. "It is light, which for thousands of years has accumulated in the earth—light

---

[1] George Stephenson (1781-1848) is known as the "Father of British Steam Railways". He is most famous for his steam-powered locomotive named *Rocket*.

which was inhaled by plants, that these during the time of their growth might fix the carbon, and which now, after having for thousands of years been buried in the coal beds of the earth, is again brought forth and set free to serve the great purpose of mankind, as here in this engine."

If the great engineer had been living today instead of in 1857, he might have asked not only "can you tell me what moves that train" but "what moves all of our trains, all of our machinery, what lights and heats our homes, our factories, our cities" and the reply would have been the same. Nothing less than the light of the sun.

The same energy of the sun takes up the water from the ocean in the form of vapor. Water would ever remain in perfect equilibrium if it were not for the action of the sun. The rays of the sun falling upon the ocean convert the water into vapor, and this vapor is taken up into the atmosphere in the form of mists. The wind gathers it together in the form of clouds and takes it across the continent. Here, through changes of temperature, it is again converted into rain or snow. So that the sun is not only the source of electrical energy by which light and heat are developed, but it is the source of life itself. No life of any kind could exist on this planet without the energizing and vitalizing magnetism derived from the sun. As the earth approaches the sun in spring, we see the result in the myriad of plants and flowers and the verdure with which the fields are covered—the life-giving force becomes everywhere apparent.

The effect of this influence is seen in the temperament of the people inhabiting the globe. When the perpendicular rays reach the people, we find a cheerful, optimistic, "sunny" disposition; but as we reach the far north where the absence of light and heat make life a struggle, we find the people correspondingly dark and gloomy.

And not only the scientist, but the poet, too, with unerring insight has recognized this all-important influence of the sunlight on the temperament of men. Over a hundred years ago, Byron thus attributed this effect to the solar orb:

> Thou chief star,
> Center of many stars! which mak'st our earth
> Endurable, and temperest the hues
> And hearts of all who walk within thy rays.
> Sire of the seasons, monarch of the climes,
> And those that dwell in them for near or far
> Our inborn spirits have a tint of thee,
> Even as our outward aspects!

All energy on this earth, organic or inorganic, is directly or indirectly derived from the sun. The flowing water, the driving wind, the passing clouds, the rolling thunder, and the flashing lightening; the falling rain, snow, dew, frost, or hail; the growth of plants, the warmth and motion of animal and human bodies, the combustion of wood, of coal—all is but solar energy in action.

The most powerful physical energy, the one whose varied forms and fields of action increase daily, whose benefits are as great as the ignorance and prejudices that reign concerning it, is beyond a shadow of doubt electric energy.

When all its modalities are known, electric energy will become the basis of therapeutics; for all other forms of energy are either merely derivatives or means of equilibrating the play of electric phenomena in the depths of our tissues.

It is by means of electric currents that we succeed best in arresting cellular disturbances. It can be applied to all diminution of energies and to every species of depression or decay in physiological vitality and to all disorders supervening in the reflex circulation.

Acting on the nervous extremities, it redresses abnormal sensibility or bridles the feverish sensations. On disordered irritability, it acts as an harmonious equalizing force, as a regenerator of the endangered vitality; and finally as a curative for perverted stability, it possesses the characteristics of militating in the same helpful and rational manner as nature, preventing our complaints from becoming chronic.

All pathology lies within its domain, and it holds a preponderant place in the treatment for rejuvenation.

In the depths of the tissues, radiant heat transforms electric energy, raises the temperature of the tissues at the precise spot indicated to it, exerting a dual influence both by its electric effects and the torrents of heat of the desired intensity with which it can flood the organ under treatment.

Applied generally, it brings to the organization a bonus in the shape of a caloric ration, which enables it to resist effectively physiological decay.

Finally, high frequency, the youngest born of electrotherapy, sees the scope of its benefactions increase daily; and in the treatment for rejuvenation, it supplies the nervous energy needful; transfusing the largest available portion of effective resistance; storing up the vital dynamism in the nervous cell.

And all this accomplished with the most absolute certainty.

To insure its efficacy, electricity must be formulated and proportioned in the same way as any other active therapeutic agent.

Electricity will act powerfully on every organ, tonify the nervous system, counterbalance the cellular exchanges, regularize failing functions, reconstruct tissues, and compel the retrogression of old age.

In static form, the entire domain of neurosis, of fears, of hypochondria, nervous and intellectual strain, over-excitement and depression, is dominated by it. All depressed or neurasthenic persons, or those who suffer from insomnia, are well acquainted with its soothing and revivifying action.

Its astounding success in all dermatological affections is well known.

Progressive regeneration, marked awakening of the digestion and the nutrition, comfort, and pleasure walking and moving, increases power or resistance to the fatigue of work, pronounced increase in the joy of living—such are the results that are generally observed.

And electricity is but another form of vibration, another name for sunshine. It is but the rays of the sun, specialized and directed. Why, then, should it not be the greatest therapeutic agent known to man is it not the source of light, of heat, of energy, of life itself?

> They drew a circle and shut me out.
> They called me a heretic, a thing to flout;
> But Love and I had the wit to win.
> We drew a circle and took them in.[1]

---

[1] Edwin Markham's "Outwitted".

SECTION ELEVEN

PERIODICITY

We live in a fathomless sea of plastic mind substance. This substance is ever alive and active. It is sensitive to the highest degree. It takes form according to mental demand. Thought forms the mould or matrix from which the substance expresses. Our ideal is the mould from which our future will emerge.

The Universe is alive. In order to express life, there must be mind; nothing can exist without mind. Everything that exists is some manifestation of this one basic substance from which and by which all things have been created and are continually being recreated. It is man's capacity to think that makes him a creator instead of a creature.

All things are the result of the thought process. Man has accomplished the seemingly impossible because he has refused to consider it impossible. By concentration, men have made the connection between the finite and the Infinite, the limited and the Unlimited, the personal and the Impersonal.

The building up of matter from electrons has been an involuntary process of individualizing, intelligent energy.

Men have learned a way to cross the ocean on floating palaces, how to fly in the air, how to transmit thought around the world on sensitized wires, how to cushion the earth with rubber, and thousands of other things just as remarkable, just as startling, and just as incomprehensible to the people of a generation ago.

Men will yet turn to the study of life itself and with the knowledge thus gained will come peace and joy and length of days.

The search for the elixir of life has always been a fascinating study and has taken hold of many minds of Utopian mould. In all times, philosophers have dreamed of the day when man will become the master of matter. Old manuscripts contain many, many receipts that have cost their investors bitter pangs of baffled disillusionment. Thousands of investigators have laid their contributions upon the sacrificial altar for the benefit of mankind.

But not through quarantine or disinfectants or boards of health will man reach the long-sought plane of physical well-being; nor by dieting or fasting or suggesting will the Elixir of Life and the Philosopher's Stone be found.

The Mercury of the Sages and the "hidden manna" are not constituents of health foods.

When man's mind is made perfect, then and then only will the body be able perfectly to express itself.

The physical body is maintained through a process of continuous destruction and reconstruction.

Health is but the equilibrium that nature maintains through the process of creating new tissue and eliminating the old, or waste, tissue.

Hate, envy, criticism, jealousy, competition, selfishness, war, suicide, and murder are the causes that produce acid conditions in the blood, causing changes which result in irritation of the brain cells, the keys upon which the soul plays "divine harmonies" or "fantastic tricks before high heaven" accordingly to the arrangement of chemical molecules in the wondrous laboratory of nature.

Birth and death are constantly taking place in the body. New cells are being created by the process of converting food, water, and air into living tissue.

Every action of the brain, every movement of the muscle, means destruction and consequent death of some of these cells, and the accumulation of these dead, unused, and waste cells is what causes pain, suffering, and disease.

We allow such destructive thoughts as fear, anger, worry, hatred, and jealousy to take possession and these thoughts influence the various functional activities of the body, the brain, the nerves, the heart, the liver, or the kidneys. They in turn refuse to perform their various functions—the constructive processes cease and the destructive processes begin.

Food, water, and air are the three essential elements necessary to sustain life, but there is something still more essential. Every time we breathe, we not only fill our lungs with air, but we fill ourselves with pranic energy, the breath of life replete with every requirement for mind and spirit.

This life giving spirit is far more necessary than air, food, or water. A man can live for forty days without food, for three days without water, and for a few minutes without air; but he cannot live a single second without ether. It is the one prime essential of life, so that the process of breathing furnishes not only food for body building, but food for mind and spirit as well.

It is a well-known fact in India, but not so well-known in this country, that in normal, rhythmical breathing, exhalation and inhalation takes place through one nostril at a time—for about one hour through the right nostril and then for a like period through the left nostril.[1]

The breath entering through the right nostril creates positive electromagnetic currents, which pass down the right side of the spine, while the breath entering through the left nostril sends negative electromagnetic currents down the left side of the spine. These currents are transmitted by way of the nerve centers of ganglia of the sympathetic nervous system to all parts of the body.

In the normal, rhythmical breath, exhalation takes about twice the time of inhalation. For instance, if inhalation requires four seconds, exhalation, including a slight natural pause before the new inhalation, requires eight seconds.

---

[1] Much more information and practical applications and exercises about proper breathing can be found in Haanel's book *The Amazing Secrets of the Yogi*, which is also published by Kallisti Publishing.

The balancing of the electromagnetic energies in the system depend to a large extent upon this rhythmical breathing, hence the importance of deep, unobstructed, rhythmic exhalation and inhalation.

Aum

The wise men of India knew that with the breath, they absorbed not only the physical elements of air, but life itself. They taught that this primary force of all forces, from which all energy is derived, ebbs and flows in rhythmical vibration through the created universe. Every living thing is alive by the virtue of partaking of this cosmic breath.

The more positive the demand, the greater the supply. Therefore, while breathing deeply and rhythmically in harmony with the universal breath, we contact the life force from the source of all life in the innermost parts of our being. Without this intimate connection of the individual soul with the great reservoir of life, existence as we know it would be an impossibility.

Freedom does not consist in the disregard of a governing principle, but in conformity to it. The laws of Nature are infinitely just. A violation of just law is not an act of freedom. The laws of Nature are infinitely beneficent. Exception from the operation of a beneficent law is not freedom. Freedom consists in conscious harmonious relation with the Laws of Being. Thus only may desire be satisfied, harmony attained, and happiness secured.

The mighty river is free only while it is confined within its banks. The banks enable it to perform its appointed function and to answer its beneficent purpose to the best advantage. While it is under the restraint of freedom, it gives out its message of harmony and prosperity. If its bed is raised or its volume greatly increased, it leaves its channel and spreads over the country, carrying a message of ruin and desolation. It is no longer free. It has ceased to be a river.

Necessities are demands and demands create action, which result in growth. This process makes for each decade a larger growth. So it is truly said that the last twenty-five years have advanced the world more than any previous century, and the last century has advanced the world more than all the ages of the past.

Notwithstanding all of the different characters, dispositions, and idiosyncrasies of different people, there is a certain definite law that dominates and governs all existence.

Thought is mind in motion, and psychic gravity is to the law of the mind what atomic attraction is to physical science. Mind has its chemistry and constituent powers and these powers are as definite as those of any physical potency.

Creation is the power of mind by which the thought is turned inward and made to impregnate and conceive new thought. It is for this reason that only the enlightened mind can think for itself.

The mind must acquire a certain character of thought, which will enable it to reproduce them itself without any seed from without to impregnate it.

When mind has acquired this nature in accordance with which thoughts are able to reproduce themselves, it is able to spontaneously generate thoughts without outside stimulation.

This is done by conceiving thought in the mind as a result of being impregnated and fecundated by the Universal.

They must not be permitted to go out into space, but on the contrary, must remain within where they will create psychic states corresponding to their natures.

It is this absorption of self-generated thoughts and their conception of corresponding psychic states that is the Principle of Causation.

This is possible owing to the fact that the mental cosmos is perpetually radiated as a unity of mind, and this mind functions in connection with the soul of man as his mind.

It being essence, it is identified with the essence of the cosmos and with the essence of all things.

The result is that having attained unto and having become an infinity of thought, the individual is omniscient in mind, omnipotent in will, and omnipresent in soul. The quality of his mind is omniscience and the quality of his soul is omnipresence.

Such a man is possessed with real power in all that he does. He is indeed a Master, the creator of his own destiny, the arbiter of his own fate.

There are many flowers of vari-coloured blossoms. Each blossomed stem simply reaches up to the great Sun—the god of vegetable life manifestation—without complaining, without doubt, in all the fullness of plant desire, faith, and expectancy. They demand and attract the richness of colour and perfume.

And so man, too, will in the future unshackle the great desire forces of mind and soul and turn them to heaven in righteous demand for the highest gift in the universe, Life.

And life means to live.

Age is a prejudice that has become so firmly anchored in your mind that any casual number of years mentioned evokes a precise image on your brain.

Twenty years, you see a youth or a young girl adorned with all of the juvenile graces.

Thirty years, a young man or young woman in the full development of vital strength and equilibrium, still on the upgrade towards the dazzling heights of maturity.

Forty years, the summit has been reached, the effort made having been maintained by the prospect of the vast horizons to be dominated.

The road traversed is contemplated with pride, but with emotion you already turn towards the abyss whose dizzy curves wind steeply into ever-increasing darkness.

Fifty years, halfway down the slope, which is still illumined by the light from the peaks though already touched by the chill of the abyss. Organism weakened and compelled to submit to numerous abdications.

Sixty years brings you to the entrance of the cold melancholy valleys. Resigned to inexorable destiny, you stand on the threshold of old age. You begin preparations for the long journey that must inevitably be undertaken.

Seventy years, wrinkled and old, endowed with numerous infirmities, you sit in the waiting room for the last journey, considering it miraculous that you are still alive.

If the eightieth year is exceeded, the fact is mentioned as an amazing phenomenon and you are treated with the respect due to antiquities.

Is this parallel correct? Is there any connection between age and age-value? Let it be emphatically stated that the tyranny of the birth certificate can be abolished.

The fact that a year represents one complete revolution of the earth around the sun has nothing in common with the evolution of the human being.

To be so many years old means simply that the circling seasons have been observed so many times, and nothing more. It implies no consideration of the intellectual or physical state. The person who has seen the untiring astronomical phenomenon forty times may be much younger in the real meaning of the word than one who has seen it but thirty times.

The vibratory activities of the planetary universe are governed by a law of periodicity. Everything that lives has periods of birth, growth, and fruitage. These periods are governed by the Septimal Law.

The Law of Sevens governs the days of the week, the phases of the moon, the harmonies of light, heat, electricity, magnetism, and atomic structure. It governs the life of individuals and of nations, and it dominates the activities of the commercial world. We can apply the same law to our own lives and therefore come into an understanding of many experiences that would otherwise appear inexplicable.

Life is growth, and growth is change. Each seven year period takes us into a new cycle. The first seven years is the period of infancy. The next seven is the period of childhood, representing the beginning of individual responsibility. The next seven represent the period of adolescence. The fourth period marks the attainment of full growth. The fifth period is the constructive period, when men acquire property, possessions, a home and family. The next, from 35-42, is a period of reactions and changes, and this in turn is followed by a period of reconstruction, adjustment, and recuperation, so as to be ready for a new cycle of sevens, beginning with the fiftieth year.

The law of periodicity governs cycles of every description. There are cycles of short periods and cycles of long periods. There are periods when the emotions gain the ascendency and the whole world is absorbed in religious thought; and there are other periods when science and learning take the ascendency and the patent office is flooded with new inventions. There are other periods when vice and crime rule with a high hand; periods of strikes and hard times; times of turmoil, confusion, and disaster; and there are periods of reform.

What is the cause of these cycles? Are they arbitrary? Have they no basis or foundation in nature, recurring with almost the regularity of clockwork and without any incentive whatsoever? Or are they perhaps due to Universal Laws and caused by the revolution of the planets in their orbits, having their origin in some principle in nature which man may learn and thus ultimately be able to predict with certainty the recurrence of the same phenomena?

The revolution of the several planets upon their axis constitutes the largest amount of matter in motion with which we are familiar, and consequently is responsible for the largest amount of energy.

The movement of the planets in their various orbits around the Sun brings the largest amount of ether under strain, and thereby brings into existence the largest amount of potential energy with which we are familiar.

All of the activities of the material universe are therefore contingent upon the movements of these several planets.

Let us note the results of these movements. The first result to be noted is the differentiation of the rays of the Sun into seven primary colours—orange, green, violet, yellow, red, indigo, and blue. These seven colours have their correspondencies in the seven notes of the musical scale.

We then find that the vibrations of each planet is responsible for the condensation or crystallization of electrons into matter, and so we have gold, silver, mercury, copper, iron, tin, and lead.

By pursuing our inquiry still further, we find that these vibrations are distributed to all parts of our body through the sympathetic nervous system, and that there are seven plexus along the spine for this purpose. We also find that there are seven functions of our body which are controlled—the heart, brain, lungs, veins, gall, liver, and spleen—and finally we find that these vibrations manifest on a still higher plane as spirit, soul, intellect, love, energy, judgement, and memory.

The angle between two planets at some time and place in their established orbits and their angular relation to the Earth causes an influence that is received by those individuals who are receptive or keyed to those particular vibrations.

Under a favourable influence, we find the body relaxed, comfortable, and at ease. This state of being reacts favourably upon the mental condition and we find mental poise, tendency to pleasure, amusement, reaction, happiness, kindness, and love.

If the influence is unfavourable, the body will be tense and irritable with corresponding mental depression, fear, anger, malice, violence, etc., according to the nature of the planets involved.

When Saturn contracts the tissues and squeezes out dead elements from the organs, Jupiter does the reverse by expanding and absorbing new elements for the maintenance of growth and development.

The effect of this Jupitarian process on the mind is to make the feelings "Jovial," optimistic, comfortable, carefree, generous, and compassionate; able to look out and beyond self to the needs and happiness of others, with the result that the word and deed bring commendation and support from others—what is done will produce fortunate results.

When Saturn is benignly aspected, the organs and functions affected by vibratory influences of that planet operate in a normal manner, but when Saturn is adversely aspected, its operations in the human body tend to inertia, contractions, restrictions, decay, or dissolution and serious disease results unless the individual is aware of what is necessary in order to counteract the influence. Herbert Spencer said, "Life is a continual adjustment of internal conditions to external environment," a statement which we all know is absolutely true, just as much as the axiom of the ancient wise men, "As above, so below." Events in the solar system have a corresponding effect in the human system. Much food for thought is furnished by the divisions of the zodiacal circle, taken in connection with the various periods of vital activity that determine the course of life.

The planet Uranus makes the circle of the heavens in eighty-four years, which is its "year"; and as this planet is one that has a special influence over man in a spiritual sense, its "month", or passage through a twelfth part of the circle, might well be expected to exercise an influence on the life of man comparable to that exhibited in the physical world by the sun during the various monthly stages of its annual course.

The fact that during each period of seven years a complete change is known to take place in the physical body, as testified to by physiologists, tends to support this theory of a sign ruling over each seven years of life; and certainly the period of eighty-four years may be taken as a life cycle, without necessarily regarding it as marking the limit of normal human life. In this sense, these eighty-four years of life will correspond to the one earth year, or to the circle of the Zodiac.

Let us now consider the division of the Zodiac into four grand quarters resembling Spring, Summer, Autumn, and Winter.

The Spring Quarter corresponds to infancy, childhood, and youth—the irresponsible and educational period from the first to the twenty-first year of life, when the personal is being fitted by service and study for the next important stage. It is the time when fidelity, filial reverence, obedience, and industry are instilled into the growing mind.

The Summer Quarter of life, from 21 to 42, is the practical period of life and is concerned with the life of the householder, in which wealth becomes an object, responsibility grows, and the duties of life become heavier and filled with business activity. It is the period when the social side of the personality is expressed and the lesson of unselfishness is learned. Prosperity comes with the fullness of life which abounds in the Summer portion. The virtues developed are caution, thrift, charity, magnanimity, diligence, and prudence.

This period of life is governed by the sign Leo, in which the life-forces burn at their greatest heat and love for partner and offspring finds its greatest height in the domestic and social world.

The Autumn Quarter of life is one in which the glory of manhood and the fullness of motherhood are turned to wider interest and personal claims are sacrificed for the benefit of those outside the narrow circle of the home. The duties of government and the national welfare are taken up with motives that are less limited and more altruistic in their nature, the desire being to help in the ruling and guiding of those who belong to the nation. The virtues to be acquired are equilibrium, justice, strength, courage, vigour, and generosity.

The concentrating power of this period is denoted by the sign Scorpio, symbol of self-controlled emotions, fixed feelings, and permanent modes of action; the fluidity and changeable sensations of the watery signs being made stable and reliable and fixed.

The next stage of life, **the Winter Quarter**, is the period in which experience is garnered and the lessons of life are stored, ready for the enriching of the ego. It is the stage in which the review of life brings wisdom and the tender feelings of sympathy to all. The virtues of the last three signs are made manifest as patience and self-sacrifice, service, purity, wisdom, gentleness, and compassion.

The centralizing of the mind in the sign Aquarius brings the climax when the man is complete, and the humanized perfection of manhood culminates in the one whose mind is wholly centered in higher states of consciousness.

This is the plan of the normal evolution of humanity, when the civilized nations have worked through their infantile, spring-like stage. For nations, like individuals, are also evolving, and it is the national good and the national perfection that is to be the outcome of this wisely ordained plan in accordance with the will of the Supreme Ruler of the Universe.

Perhaps it was this national good and national perfection that one of our great men saw when he had the wonderful vision that he so beautifully described.

"A vision of the future arises. I see a world where thrones have crumbled and where kings are dust. The aristocracy of idleness has perished from the earth.

"I see a world without a slave. Man at last is free. Nature's forces have by science been enslaved. Lightening and light, wind and waves, frost and flames, and all the subtle powers of the earth and air are the tireless toilers for the human race.

"I see a world at peace, adorned with every form of art, with music's myriad voices thrilled, while lips are rich with words of love and truth; a world in which no exile sighs, no prisoner mourns; a world in which the gibbet's shadow does not fall; a world where labour reaps its full reward, where work and worth go hand in hand.

"I see a world without the beggar's outstretched palm, the miser's heartless stony stare, the piteous wail of want, the livid lips of lies, the cruel eyes of scorn.

"I see a race without disease of flesh or brain—shapely and fair, married harmony of form and function—and, as I look, life lengthens, joy deepens, love canopies the earth; and over all, in the great dome, shines the eternal star of faith."[1]

---

[1] From "A Vision of War" by Robert G. Ingersoll (1833-1899). Ingersoll was the foremost orator and political speechmaker of late 19th century America.

A Book About You

Section Twelve

The Source of Life

Life is not created—it simply is. All nature is animate with this force we call "Life." The phenomena of life on this physical plane, with which we are chiefly concerned, are produced by the involution of "energy" into "matter," and matter is, itself, an involution of energy.

Living tissue is organized or organic life; dead tissue is unorganized or inorganic matter. When life disappears from an organism, disintegration begins, the process of organization ceases.

Organization requires a high rate of vibration, or short wave length, moving with great intensity. The molecules of which the tissue is composed are in a continuous state of activity. The result is the tissues manifest what we call life.

Life vibrations have but one source and that is the Sun. Senility is a part of the death process. It is caused by the accumulation of earthy salts or so-called mineral matter.

This mineral matter usually consists of lime and chalk that settles upon the walls of the arteries, which become hardened and calcinous and lose their elasticity.

If the vibrations are sufficiently intense, it would be impossible for these salts to settle in the system. The intense vibration would make the accumulation impossible; the minerals would be expelled in the process of elimination.

Old age, decay, and death are therefore simply due to the inability of the individual to keep in tune with the vibrations from the Sun, which is the source of all life.

Longevity and vitality are in direct ratio as we contact the intense vibrations from the Sun and isolate ourselves from the slow, disorganized, disintegrating, and deathly vibrations of the Earth.

Life is a rate of vibration, a mode of motion; death is the absence of that vibration.

Life is a manifestation of activity. Death is the process of disintegration, the absence of activity. The vibrations of life originate in the Sun. The vibrations of death originate in the Earth.

The Sun is the source of life, the Moon of form, and the Earth of disintegration or death. The Earth is ever seeking to embrace in its bosom all things; it is the tomb or fixed resting place for every form of organized manifestation.

The vibrations from the Earth are, therefore, the vibrations of destruction, of disintegration. Nothing has so far been able to resist the continual pull of these Earthy vibrations; everything has had to finally succumb, all form of whatever nature has thus far been compelled to return to the Earth to await the vitalizing vibrations of the Sun before being again brought into manifestation.

But, will this always be true? Not necessarily. It may not always be necessary to contact these disintegrating vibrations. We may be able to insulate ourselves to some extent at least.

The Universe was built by vibration; that is to say, the specific form that everything has, on wither a large or a small scale, is due absolutely to the specific rate of vibration that gave expression to it. The Universe, then, both in general and in particular, is the effect of a system of vibration. In other words, the music of the spheres has expressed itself in that form which we denominate the Cosmos.

This vibration expresses intelligence. This is not intelligence as we understand the word, but a cosmic knowledge which is responsible for the growth of finger nails, hair, bones, teeth, and skin, the circulation of blood, and breathing, which proceed whether we are asleep or awake.

Thus, consciousness or intelligence abounds in every thing, peculiar only to itself only in that it differs in character to every other thing; for there is but one Universal consciousness or intelligence, while there are multitudinous different expressions of it. The rock, the fish, the animal, the human are all recipients of the one Universal intelligence. They are only differently formed manifestations of Cosmic substance—differently combined rates of motion or vibration.

Mind is a system of vibration. The brain is the vibrator and thought is the organized effect of each particular vibration when expressed through the requisite combination of cells.

It is not the number of the cells, but their vibratory adaptability which gives range to the thoughts of which the mind is capable.

It is through the Universal Mind that the "seeds of thought" enter the brain of man, so that it conceives thought which becomes a current of energy, centripetal in the mind of man and centrifugal in the Universal Mind.

These seeds of thought have a tendency to germinate, to sprout, and to grow; they thus form that we call ideas.

When a mental picture is formed in the brain, the rate of vibration corresponding to that picture is immediately awakened in the ether. It depends, however, upon whether the Will or Desire principle is acting as to whether that vibration moves inward or outward.

If the Will is used, the vibration moves outward and the principle of force is put into operation. If the Desire nature is awakened, the vibrations move inward and the Law of Attraction is put into operation.

In either case, the Law of Causation expresses itself through the embodying of creative principle.

The time is not far distant when man will be able to make the body immune against disease and arrest the ordinary process of old age and physical decay—perpetuate youth even after the body has passed the mark of the centuries.

Immortality, or perpetual life, is the fondest hope, the legitimate goal and just birthright of every human being. But the majority of people of all religions, and those of no religious belief at all, seem to think that it is to be attained, if at all, at some future time and on some other plane of existence.

Every human being who is not sick or insane, has an innate desire to live as long as possible. If there is an individual person in the world who does not desire to live, it is because he is in some abnormal condition of body or mind or expects to be.

As a matter of fact, the more highly enlightened and developed the individual, the more intense the desire and longing for life, and it is improbable that there would be a natural desire for something that was impossible of attainment.

Prof. Jaques Loeb, formerly of the Department of Psychology at the University of California, said several years ago, "Man will live forever when he has learned to establish the right protoplasmic reaction to the body."

Thomas Edison says, "I have many reasons to believe that the time will come when man will not die."

Five-sevenths of the flesh and blood are water, while the substance of the body consists of albumen, fibrin, cassein, and gelatin; that is, organic substance composed originally of four essential gases—oxygen, nitrogen, hydrogen, and carbonic acid.

Water is a combination of two gases and air is a mixture of three gases. Thus, our bodies are composed of only transformed gases. None of our flesh existed three or four months ago; face, mouth, arms, hair, even the very nails. The entire organism is but a current of molecules, a ceaselessly renewed flame, a stream at which we may look all of our lives and never see the same water again.

These molecules do not touch each other and are continually renewed by means of assimilation—directed, governed, and organized by the immaterial force that animates it.

To this force we may give the name "soul", so writes the great French astronomer, physicist, biologist, and metaphysician Camille

Flammarion.

The Bridge of Life, a symbol of physical regenesis, has been exploited in song, drama, and story. Paracelsus, Pythagorus, Lycurgus, Valentin, Wagner, and a long unbroken line of the Illuminati from time immemorial have chanted their epics in unison with this "riddle of the Sphinx", across the scroll of which is written, "Solve me or die."

This solution may lie in an understanding of the nature of the glands that control physical and mental growth, and all metabolic processes of fundamental importance.

These glands dominate all the vital functions and cooperate in an intimate relationship which may be compared to an interlocking directorate.

They furnish the internal secretions or hormones which determine whether we are to be tall or short, handsome or homely, brilliant or dull, cross or congenial.

Sir William Osler, one of the world's great thinkers, said, "For man's body is a humming hive of working cells each with its specific functions, all under central control of the brain and heart, and all dependent on secretions from the glands which lubricate the wheels of life. For example, remove the thyroid gland just below the Adam's apple, and you deprive man of the lubricants which enable his thought-engines to work, and gradually the stored acquisitions of his mind cease to be available, and within a year he sinks into dementia. The normal processes of the skin cease, and the hair falls, the features bloat, and the paragon of animals is transformed into a shapeless caricature of humanity."

There are seven major glands: the pituitary, the thyroid, the pancreas, the adrenal, the pineal, the thymus, and the sex glands. They control the metabolism of the body and dominate all vital functions.

The **pituitary gland** is a small gland located near the center of the head, directly under the third ventricle of the brain where it rests in a depression in the bony floor-plate of the skull. Its secretions have an important part in the mobilizing of carbohydrates, maintaining blood pressure, stimulating the other glands, and maintaining the tonicity of the sympathetic nerve system.

The **thyroid gland** is located at the frontal base of the neck, extending upward in a sort of semicircle on both sides. The thyroid secretion is important in mobilizing both proteids and carbohydrates; it stimulates other glands, helps resist infections, affects the hair growth, and influences the organs of the digestion and elimination. It is a strongly determining factor in the all-around physical development, and also in the mental functioning. A well-balanced thyroid will insure an active, efficient, and smoothly coordinated mind and body.

The **adrenal glands** are located just above the small of the back. These organs have sometimes been called the "beauty glands", since one of their functions is to keep the pigments of the body in proper solution and distribution. But of greater importance is the agency of the adrenal secretion in other directions. The secretions contain a most valuable blood pressure agent and are a tonic to the sympathetic nerve system, hence to the involuntary muscles, heart, arteries, and intestines. These glands respond to certain emotional excitements by an immediate increase in volume of secretion, thus increasing the energy of the whole system and preparing it for effective purpose.

The **pineal gland** is a small conical structure located behind the third ventricle of the brain. The ancients realized that this gland was of vast importance—it is spoken of as a spiritual center, the seat of the soul, and possibly of eternal youth or everlasting life. It is near the top and at the back of the head.

The **thymus gland** is located at or near the bottom of the throat, just below the thyroid gland. It is considered essential for children only, but is ti not possible that the degeneration of this gland is one of the causes of premature senility?

The **pancreas** is located just behind the peritoneum near the stomach. This gland aids digestion and when not properly functioning, an excess of sugar may be produced, which causes diabetes and other serious troubles.

The **sex glands** are located at the lower part of he abdomen. It is through the functioning of these glands that life is created and the process of reproduction carried on.

When the secretions from these glands are not called upon for procreative purposes, they are poured into the cell life, renewing energy, strength, and vitality.

If they fail to function, there is depression and general debility.

It is clear then, that if we can find some way to make these glands continue to function, we can renew our health, strength, and youth indefinitely; because the thyroid develops vital energy, the pituitary controls blood pressure and develops mental energy, the pancreas controls digestion and bodily vigor, the adrenals furnish pep and ambition, and the sex glands control the secretions that manifest as youth, strength, and power.

We can better understand the mechanism of glands when we remember that the Sun is the source of all life; that the rays from the Sun are differentiated into seven different tones or colours or qualities by the seven different planets, and that they enter the human system by the seven plexi located along the spinal column, and we now find that this life is carried on to the seven major glands in the body, where it controls and dominates every function of life.

Unfortunately, however, ordinary window glass excludes practically all of the ultraviolet rays, which are the most essential in the maintenance of health and vitality. A few sanitariums and hospitals have had special windows of fused quartz constructed, which admits ultraviolet rays, but so far the cost of such windows are prohibitive, a single window costing from ten thousand to fifteen thousand dollars.

Apparatus is now constructed, however, that may be attached to the ordinary electric current, so that the full benefit of the vital rays from the solar orb may be secured.

When the glands are supplied with the vital rays of which we have heretofore been deprived, the result will be a remarkable degree of vitality and mental and physical vigor. In fact, it is already known that cholesterol can be converted into a vitamin by the action of the ultraviolet rays, and it is possible that other inert substances may be activated in like manner.

The ultrared rays have also been found to be an exceedingly valuable therapeutic agent. Fabrics of certain weaves are used to filter these rays.

Deductions from the experiments made by several of the world's leading scientists more than fifteen years ago are to the effect that it will be possible for the physical body of man to become so purified and responsive that it may continue living from age to age without death. The income and outgo of the body can be so perfectly adjusted, that the organism will not become old, but will be rebuilt from day to day.

The vibratory force of Life can be inspired to such a degree and radiated through the tissue to such an extent that this man of clay will really become a temple of the living God, not merely a reservoir of unconscious and unregulated intelligence.

By very simple hygienic care, we can greatly prolong each life manifestation. Hence, we have reason to believe that a complete knowledge of vibratory force and its effect upon the structure of the body will aid the organism in making the life manifestations permanent.

Death is not a necessary, inevitable consequence or attribute of life; death is biologically a relatively new thing, which made its appearance only after living things had advanced a long way on the path of evolution.

Single-celled organisms have proved, under critical experimental observation, to be immortal. They reproduce by simple fission of the body, one individual becoming two. This process may go on indefinitely, without any permanent slacking of the rate of cell division and without the intervention of a rejuvenating process, provided the environment of the cells is kept favourable. The germ cells of all sexually differentiated organisms are, in a similar sense, immortal. Reduced to a formula, we may say that the fertilized ovum produces a soma and more germ cells. The soma eventually dies. Some of the germ cells prior to that event produced somata and germ cells, and so on in a continuous cycle that has never yet ended since the appearance of multi-cellular organisms on the earth.

So long as reproduction goes on in this way in these multi-cellular forms, there is no place for death.

The successful cultivation of the tissues of higher vertebrates over an indefinitely long period of time demonstrates that death is in no sense a necessary concomitant of cellular life.

It may fairly be said that the potential immortality of all essential cellular elements of the body either has been fully demonstrated or has been carried far enough to make the probability very great. Generalizing the results of the tissue culture work of the last two decades, it is highly probable that the cells of all the essential tissues of the metazoan body are potentially immortal when placed separately under such conditions as to supply appropriate food in the right amount and to remove promptly the deleterious products of metabolism.

A fundamental reason why the higher multi-cellular animals do not live forever appears to be that in the differentiation and specialization of function of cells and tissues in the body as a whole, any individual part does not find the conditions necessary for its continued existence. In the body, any part is dependent for the necessities of its existence upon other parts or upon the organization of the body as a whole. It is the differentiation and specialization of function of the mutually dependent aggregate of cells and tissues that constitute the metazoan body that brings about death, and not any inherent or inevitable mortal process in the individual cells themselves.

When cells show characteristic senescent changes, it is probably a consequence of their mutually dependent association in the body as a whole. It does not primarily originate in any particular cell because of the fact that the cell is old, it occurs in the cells when they are removed from the mutually dependent relationship of the organized body as a whole. In short, death does not appear to be a primary attribute of the psychological economy of individual cells as such, but rather of the body as a whole.

Recent researches have shown conclusively that tissue and cells in the human body need not necessarily decay. Formerly, it was thought that there was no way to ward off senility and that cells are bound to break down due to old age, which simply means wear and tear. This, however, in the light of modern science, is no longer countenanced. The study of gland science has convinced many physicists that the human cells can be rejuvenated or replaced continuously and that such a thing as old age can be warded off for several hundred years.

It is well known that it takes a lifetime to gain valuable experience. Men at the head of great industries frequently are over sixty years of age, and their advice is sought because they have gained most valuable experience during all those years. It would seem, therefore, important to lengthen the span of life and, indeed, present indications are that this can and will be done.

Some of our best authorities see no reason why a human being should not attain the age of several hundred years; not as some extraordinary feat, but considered as a fair average. There are, of course, people now living who are 125 years old, but these are, naturally, exceptions. Medical scientists assert that the goal of 200 years will be reached some day in the future. When we stop to think that the average lifetime used to be 40 years and that we now consider the man of 50 years to be in the prime of his life, who knows but that fifty years hence a man in his prime will be 100 or 150 years of age.

Dr. Monroe, an eminent physician and scientist of Great Britain, says, "The human frame as a machine contains within itself no marks by which we can possibly predict it decay; it is apparently intended to go on forever."

But of all the multiple adepts or masters that have kept the light burning above the Three Piers of the magical Bridge, none has more clearly and beautifully written thereof than did the great poet Isaiah:

> "Then the eyes of the blind shall be opened and
> the ears of the deaf shall be unstopped. Then
> shall the lame man leap as a hart, and the tongue
> of the dumb shall sing; for in the wilderness shall
> waters break out, and streams in the desert. And
> the glowing sand shall become a pool, and the
> thirsty ground springs of water; in the habita-
> tions of jackals, where they lay shall be grass
> with reeds and bushes. And a highway shall be
> there, and a way and it shall be called "The Way
> of Holiness;" the unclean shall not pass over it,
> but it shall be for the redeemed. The wayfaring
> man, yea, fools, shall not err therein."

The nerves are fine threads of different colours, each one having a special chemical affinity for certain organic substances—oil or albu-men—through and by which the organism is materialized and the process of life carried on.

The imagination might easily conceive that these delicate infini-tesimal fibers are strings of the Human Harp, and that the molecular minerals are the fingers of Infinite Energy striking the notes of some Divine Anthem.

THE VIEW

Looked on the World with a care-lined frown
Mottled and grey were the shaded ways;
Anger and Avarice, Envy and Hate,
Clouded the view of the sun-draped days.

Looked on the World with a Soulful Song,
Zephyrs blew sweet o'er the Hills of Time;
Wafted the Peace I had longed for long—
Sundrift aglow on the fields of Thyme.

Follow the THOUGHT and the THOUGHT SUBLIME
Shines through the dark and the darkness fades
THOUGHTS are the THINGS that control the CHIMES
Of the Bells that Ring in the GOLDEN GLADES.

—Nate Collier

Section Thirteen

The Emotions

Your emotions will invariably seek to express themselves in action. The emotion of love will therefore seek expression in demonstrations of loving service.

Emotions of hate will seek expression in vindictive or hostile actions.

Emotions of shame will seek expressions in actions corresponding to the nature of the cause that brought the emotion into being.

Emotions of sorrow will bring the tear ducts into violent action.

From this you will see that the emotions always focalize the energies upon the idea or desire that is seeking an outlet.

When the emotions find an outlet through the proper channel, all is well; but if they are forbidden or repressed, the desire or wish will continue to gather energy and if, for any reason, it is finally suppressed, it will pass into the subconscious where it will remain.

Such a suppressed emotion becomes a complex. Such a complex is a living thing—it has vital power and force and the vital force retains its intensity undiminished throughout the entire lifetime unless released. In fact, it gains in violence with every similar thought, desire, wish, or memory.

The emotion of love causes the solar plexus to become active, which in turn influences the action of glands which produce a vibratory effect on certain organs of the body which creates passion. The emotion of hate causes an acceleration of certain bodily activities, which change the chemical organization of the blood and eventuates in semi-paralysis or, if long continued, in complete paralysis.

Emotions may be expressed through mental, verbal, or physical action, and they usually find expression in one of these three ways and are therefore released and this energy dissipated in a few hours; but when by reason of honour, pride, anger, hatred, or bitterness, these emotions are buried from consciousness, they become mental abscesses in the subconscious realm and cause bitter suffering.

Such a complex may find reverse expression. For instance, a man who has been forbidden to express his love for a woman may develop into a woman hater. He may be irritated and annoyed by the very sight of feminine things. He may appear to be bold, independent, and domineering, but this will be but the camouflage by which he is attempting to cover up the craving for love and sympathy that has been denied him.

Should this man eventually select a mate, he will unconsciously select one of an opposite type to the one who caused him sorrow. The attachment has been reversed—he wants no reminders.

Suffering is an emotion and it opens the doors of the subconscious mind. The thought "this is what I get for wrong-doing" produces a conclusion—"Well, I'll never do that again!" This is the reformation suggestion that goes down into the subconscious mind by the auto-suggestion of the individual suffering penance. Thus, reformation takes place because it changes the soul's desire, and also produces a new desire to avoid the consequences of suffering indicated to it by the penance.

Desire originates in the subconscious mind. It is plainly an emotion. Emotion originates in the soul or subconscious mind. Pleasure emotions are the diversions and rewards for service which the subconscious mind renders the body.

You have seen that when any thought, idea, or purpose finds its way into the subconscious through the emotions, the sympathetic nervous system takes up the thought, idea, or purpose and carries it to every part of the body, thus converting the idea, thought, or purpose into an actual experience in your life.

The necessary interaction of the conscious and subconscious mind requires a similar interaction between the corresponding system of nerves. The cerebrospinal system is the organ of the conscious mind and the sympathetic is the organ of the subconscious. The cerebro-spinal system is the channel through which we receive conscious perception from the physical senses and exercise control over the movements of the body. This system of nerves has its center in the brain.

The sympathetic system has its center in a ganglionic mass at the back of the stomach known as the solar plexus and is the channel of that mental action which unconsciously supports the vital functions of the body.

The connection between the two systems is made by the vagus nerve, which passes out of the cerebral region as a portion of the voluntary system of the thorax, sending out branches to the heart and lungs, and finally passing through the diaphragm it loses its outer coating and becomes identified with the nerves of the sympathetic system, so forming a connecting link between the two and making man physically a single entity.

The solar plexus has been likened to the sun of the body, because it is a central point of distribution for the energy that the body is constantly generating. This energy is a very real energy, and this sun is a very real sun, and the energy is being distributed by very real nerves to all parts of the body and is thrown off in an atmosphere which envelopes the body.

If this radiation is sufficiently strong, the person is called magnetic; he is said to have a strong personality. Such a person may wield an immense power for good; his presence alone will often bring comfort to the troubled minds with which he comes in contact.

When the solar plexus is in active operation and is radiating life and energy and vitality to every part of the body and to every one that we meet, the sensations are pleasant, the body is filled with health, and all with whom we come in contact experience a pleasant sensation.

If there is any interruption of this radiation, the sensations are unpleasant, the flow of vitality and energy to some part of the body is stopped, and this is the cause of every ill to the human race—physical, mental, or environmental.

Any explanation of the phenomena of life must be based upon the theory of Oneness. The psychic element being found within all living substance, this Cosmic Intelligence must have existed before living substance could have come into existence and, therefore, it exists today all around us, flowing in and through us. This Cosmic Consciousness projects itself in the form of living substance and it acts with a conscious intelligence in manufacturing its food supply and evolving organizations on to a higher and higher plane of life.

This Cosmic Mind is the creative Principle of the Universe, the Divine Essence of all things. It is, therefore, a subconscious activity and all subconscious activities are governed by the sympathetic nervous system, which is the organ of the subconscious mind.

No human intelligence has ever accomplished the results that the Cosmic Intelligence produced in developing a chemical laboratory right within the foundation of plant life, and the production of elaborate mechanical devices and harmonious social organization right within our own bodies.

In the mineral world everything is solid and fixed. In the animal and vegetable kingdom, it is in a state of flux, forever changing, always being created and recreated. In the atmosphere we find heat, light, and energy. Each realm becomes finer and more spiritual as we pass from the visible to the invisible, from the coarse to the fine, from the low potentiality to high potentiality. When we reach the invisible, we find energy in its purest and most volatile state.

And as the most powerful forces of Nature are the invisible forces, so we find that the most powerful forces of man are his invisible forces, his spiritual force. And the only way in which the spiritual force can manifest is through the process of thinking.

Addition and subtraction are, therefore, spiritual transactions; reasoning is a spiritual process; ideas are spiritual conceptions; questions are spiritual searchlights; and logic, argument, and philosophy are spiritual machinery.

Every thought brings into action certain physical tissue—parts of the brain, nerve, or muscle. This produces an actual physical change in the construction of the tissue. Therefore, it is only necessary to have a certain number of thoughts on a given subject in order to bring about a complete change in your physical organization.

Thoughts of courage, power, and inspiration will eventually take root, and as this takes place, you will see life in a new light. Life will have a new meaning for you. You will be reconstructed and filled with joy, confidence, hope, and energy. You will see opportunities to which you were heretofore blind. You will recognize possibilities which before had no meaning for you. The thoughts with which you have been impregnated are radiated to those around you, and they in turn help you onward and upward; you attract to yourself new associates, and this in turn changes your environment; so that by this simple exercise of thought, you change not only yourself, but your environment, circumstances, and conditions.

These changes are brought about by the psychic element of life. This psychic element is not mechanical; because of its power of selection, organization, and direction, such a power cannot be automatically mechanical.

The Cosmic Intelligence possesses the function of memory for the purpose of recording all the experiences which it encounters and projecting and organizing itself on higher planes of life. It is this function of memory which is the hereditary directing force found within living organisms.

This hereditary directing force frequently manifests as fear. Fear is an emotion; it is consequently not amenable to reason. You may therefore fear your friends as well as your enemies, fear the present and past as well as the future; if fear attacks you, it must be destroyed.

You will be interested in knowing how to accomplish this. Reason will not help you at all, because fear is a subconscious thought, a product of the emotions. There must then be some other way.

The way is to awaken the Solar Plexus, get it into action. If you have practiced deep breathing, you can expand the abdomen to the limit. That is the first thing to do; hold this breath for a second or two, then still holding it, draw in more air and carry it to the upper chest, drawing in the abdomen.

This effort flushes the face red. Hold this breath also for a second or two and then still holding this breath, deflate the chest and expand the abdomen again. Do not exhale this breath at all, but, still holding it, alternately expand the abdomen and chest rapidly some four or five times. Then exhale. The fear is gone.

If the fear does not leave you at once, repeat the process until it does. It will not be long before you are feeling entirely normal. Why? Because, in the first place, this breathing effort concentrated at the pit of the stomach affects the great ganglion of the sympathetic nervous system lying exactly opposite, called the Solar Plexus, which largely governs circulation.

The stimulation of the Solar Plexus releases the nerve currents and the renewed circulation reestablishes the muscular control.

The breath entering through the right nostril creates positive electromagnetic currents, which pass down the right side of the spine; while the breath entering through the left nostril sends negative electromagnetic currents down the left side of the spine. These currents are transmitted by way of the nerve centers or ganglia of the sympathetic nervous system.

All force or energy comes from the sun. We may be said to literally live, move, and have our being, in a physical sense, in the sun. This force or energy enters the etheric spleen with every inhalation of the breath. As it enters the spleen, the solar plexus draws it to itself with every exhalation, and from the solar plexus it travels along the nerves to the sacrum plexus situated at the extreme end of the spine, and to the cardinal plexus, the core of the brain. These are the three main centers of the body.

From the cardinal plexus, this life energy traverses the nerves to the head. Again on the downward path, it passes through to the psychic center, situated between the two eyebrows. Then it traverses the nerves of the face; then the bronchial center; the throat front; the pulmonary center; the upper chest and the lungs; the lower lung center, seated above the heart; the vital and generatic center seated at the base of the stomach; and so this life energy makes the circuit of the nerves until it gradually works its way out through the pores of the skin.

You will therefore readily see why this exercise can and does completely eliminate that arch enemy Fear.

If you are tired, if you wish to conquer fatigue, stand still wherever you may be with your feet holding all your weight. Inhale deeply, raise the body on the tip toes with the hands stretched above the head and the fingers pointed upward. Bring your hands together above the head, inhaling slowly and exhaling violently. Repeat this exercise three times. It will only take a minute or two and you will feel more refreshed than you would if you took a nap, and in time you will be able to overcome the tendency to fatigue.

The virtue of this exercise is in the intention. The intention governs the attention. This in turn acts upon the imagination; the imagination is a form of thought, which in turn is mind in motion.

All thought formations interact upon one another until they come to a state of maturity, where they reproduce their kind. This is the law of creation. These are indicated in the characteristics of the individual. If the body is large, the bones heavy, the finger nails thick, the hair coarse, then we know that the physical dominates. If the body is slight, the bones small, the finger nails thin and pliable, then we know that the mental and spiritual characteristics prevail. Coarse hair indicates materialistic tendencies. Fine hair indicates sensitive and discriminating mental qualities. Straight hair indicates directness of character. Curly hair indicates changefulness and uncertainty in thought.

Blue eyes indicate a light, happy, cheerful, active disposition. Grey eyes indicate a cool, calculating, determined disposition. Black eyes indicate a quick, nervous, venturesome disposition. Brown eyes indicate sincerity, energy, and affection.

You are, therefore, a complete manifestation of your most inward thoughts. The colour of your eyes, the texture of your hair, the quality of your hair, every line and curve of your body are indications of the character of the thought that you habitually entertain.

Not only this, but the letters which you write carry not only the message that the words contain, but they are charged with an energy corresponding with the nature of your thought and, therefore, often bring a very different message than the one which you intended to send.

And finally, even the clothes which you wear eventually take on the mental atmosphere which surrounds you, so that the trained psychometrist finds no difficulty in reading the character of those who have worn a garment for any length of time.

YOU

I feel your brow, your hair,
You do not know that I am there.
Could you but know—Oh, joy sublime,
What then were place or space or time!

SECTION FOURTEEN

MAGNETISM

In an ordinary bar of iron or steel, the molecules arrange themselves promiscuously in the body. The magnetic circuits are satisfied internally and there is no resulting external magnetism.

When the bar is magnetized, the molecules rearrange themselves according to the law of attraction, turn on their axis, and resume positions more nearly in a straight line with their north ends pointing the same way. The closed magnetic circuits are thus broken up and external magnetism made evident.

You cannot see the molecules of iron or steel changing their relative positions under the influence of magnetism, but the effect reveals the change that has taken place. When all of the molecules have turned on their axis until they are all arranged symmetrically, the bar has been completely magnetized. It cannot be further influenced, however strong the force.

The bar has now become a magnet and will exert force in every direction. The amount of force that the magnet will exert decreases as the distance from the magnet increases.

The magnetic lines complete their circuits independently—and never cut, cross, or merge into each other.

Another bar of iron or steel placed in the magnetic field of a magnet assumes the properties of the magnet; this phenomena is known as magnetic induction. This is the action and reaction which always precedes the attraction of a magnet for a magnetic body.

Electricity is the invisible agent known to us by its various manifestations. You are a perfect electrical plant. Food, water, and air furnish the fuel, the solar plexus is the storage battery, and the sympathetic nervous system is the medium by which the body is charged with magnetism. Sleep is the process by which the battery is recharged and the vital processes replenished and renewed.

The male is the positive or electrical charge and the female is the negative or magnetic charge. The male represents current, force, energy; the female capacity, resistance, and power.

What happens when one of the opposite sex comes into your magnetic field? First, the Law of Attraction is brought into operation; then, by the process of induction, you are magnetized and assume the properties of the person whom you are contacting.

When another person enters your magnetic field, what is it that passes from one to the other? What causes the thrill and tingle over the entire sympathetic nervous system? It is the cells rearranging themselves so as to carry the charge of energy, life, and vitality that is passing from one to the other, and which you are receiving by the process of induction.

You are being magnetized and in this process you are assuming the qualities and characteristics of the person whom you are contacting.

In the magnetism which is passing from person to person is all the joy, all the sorrow, all the love, the hatred, the music, the art, the fear, the suffering, the success, the defeat, the ambition, the triumph, the reverence, the courage, the wisdom, the virtue, the beauty, which heredity and environment have stored in the life of your love; for it is nothing less than love, this Law of Attraction is the Law of Love; and Love is life, and this is the experience by which life is being quickened into action, by which character, heredity, and destiny are being determined.

When you become impregnated with these thoughts of love, of success, of ambition, of triumph, of defeat, of sorrow, of hatred, of fear, or of suffering, are you immediately conscious of them? By no means. Why not? The reply is very simple and easily understood. The brain is the organ of the conscious mind, and it has five methods only by which it can contact the objective world. These methods are the five senses: seeing, hearing, smelling, tasting, and feeling. But Love is something which we cannot see, we cannot hear, neither can we taste, smell, or touch it. It is therefore plainly a subconscious activity or emotion. The subconscious, however, has its own system of nerves whereby it contacts every part of the body and receives sensations from the outer world, the mechanism is complete, it controls all of the vital processes: the heart, the lungs, the digestion, the kidneys, the liver, the organs of generation. Nature has evidently taken all of these out of the control of the conscious mind and placed them in the control of the more reliable subconscious, where there can be no interference.

Where physical contact is made, an entirely different situation is created. In this case, we bring into action the cerebrospinal nervous system also through the sense of touch. You will remember that the conscious mind has five methods by which it contacts the outer world; the sense of touch is one of these. So that actual physical contact brings into action not only the sympathetic nervous system, but the cerebrospinal nervous system also.

As the brain is the organ of this system of nerves, you immediately become conscious of any such action. So that when both the emotions and the feelings are aroused by both mental and physical contact, we bring into action every nerve of the body.

The exchange resultant from these associations should be beneficial, inspiring, and vitalizing, and such is the case when the association is ideal and constructive. Such an association produces and effect in consciousness and life, typified by the increased power and usefulness in the crossing of plants, birds, and animals. This result means added power, utility, beauty, wealth, or worth.

The Principle of Attraction as it operates through infinite time, evidences itself in the form of growth. The one fundamental and inevitable result of attraction is the bringing together of things that have an affinity for each other with a resultant eternally advancing growth of life.

You have found what happens when one of the opposite sex comes into your magnetic field. Now let us consider what happens when you approach another personality of the same sex.

All human intercourse is a matter of accumulation, and you will be a factor in determining what the relationship shall be and it rests with you to determine whether you shall be the predominant factor in the new relationship.

If you give, you are the positive or predominant factor.

If you receive, you are the negative or receptive factor.

Each person is a magnet having both positive and negative poles, and with tendencies that impel an automatic sympathy with or antipathy toward whatever approaches or is approached.

Normally, the positive poles lead the way, and the approach of two positives from opposite directions foreshadows a collision.

The fundamental of life is harmony and discords are obstructions that lie in your path. The obscure the reality of peace that lies at the heart of every experience, but as you increase in experience, you are enabled to discern the good in apparent evil and your power of attraction increases proportionally.

To the extent that you are magnetized toward "saturation point" you may determine your relation to others and their relation to you.

Any magnet has the power to induce harmonious conjunction with one that is less powerful.

This is accomplished by causing a reversal of polarity of one of the magnets. Then dissimilar poles come together in peace and harmony.

The more positive magnet will compel the less positive magnet to become receptive to the greater power that dominates it.

The lesser magnet may be obliged to be receptive to the overpowering influence. It acknowledges the impelling power that requires it to reverse its polarity.

It turns its positive pole away and its negative pole toward the positive pole of the greater magnet, and the two meet in harmonious relation.

The negative magnet may, however, have the higher knowledge and may not desire to dominate. Possessing greater wisdom, it may disdain the use of force.

Perhaps it prefers to conciliate or wishes to receive rather than give. Instead of forcibly obliging the lesser magnet to accommodate itself to imposed conditions, the greater magnet may voluntarily reverse its own polarity.

If you are a great soul, you will know intuitively whether to exercise coercion or nonresistance. Where coercion is used, the resultant harmony is an involuntary and temporary submission; while the non-resistant method binds because of the sense of freedom that it confers.

The coercive method is distinctly intellectual, while that of non-resistance is essentially spiritual.

If you are highly developed spiritually and similarly endowed with intellectual power, you can use the latter to the greatest advantage. In this case, you will neither discard reason or logic because in your understanding of life's mathematics, you will make application of spiritual geometry, mental algebra, or physical arithmetic according to the requirements of your problem.

You will find that existence involves ever recurrent occasions for accommodation, compromise, and reversal of polarities. You may escape compulsion through acquiescent submission and avoid the use of force by inviting pleasurable acquiescence.

You may command and exact unwilling obedience or you may invite and receive voluntary cooperation.

You may induce harmonies and create friendships or you may plant hatreds that will react as obligations that must eventually be satisfied.

An understanding of the properties of the human magnet will enable you to solve many of the problems of life.

Conflict and opposition have their places, but ordinarily they constitute obstacles and pitfalls to be avoided.

You will find that you can always avoid useless opposition and unprofitable conflict by reversing your polarity or impelling its reversal in your would-be opponent.

You are, indeed, in the loving care of principles that are immutable and that are designed solely for your benefit.

You may place yourself in harmony with them and thus express a life of comparative peace and happiness, or you may put yourselves in opposition to the inevitable with necessarily unpleasant results.

You determine your conscious relation to all that is. You express the exact degree of happiness or the reverse that you have earned through the associations which you have permitted to come into your life.

You may, from any one experience, learn the spiritual lesson it was intended to convey or you may make necessary many similar experiences.

You may gather wisdom from experiences rapidly and with ease, or you may do so slowly and with difficulty.

You are able to consciously control your conditions as you come to sense the purposes of what you attract and are able to extract from each experience that which you require for further growth.

When you possess this faculty to a high degree, you may grow rapidly and reach planes of thought where opportunities for greater service await you.

It remains for you on each successive plane to learn how to express the greater harmonies that your higher growth has placed within you reach, for it is only through expression that you may appropriate what is for your use or benefit.

You have now entered upon the borderland of the basic, the fundamental, the active principle of life. Little did you realize a few years ago the innumerable vibrations that surround you such as electric, magnetic, heat, and actinic; the control and the use of which are now keeping you busy.

Suppose that what you term "electrons" should be active centers of intelligence connected with an Infinite Mind, which is all-wise and all-knowing. That marvelous mind that thinks with design and sees ends from beginnings.

Suppose that "electrons" should not be centers of force and energy only, but centers of intelligence and that mankind will finally discover that the brain is an organized center of millions of these intelligent electrons and that they are in contact with all other electrons of which the Universe is composed.

The Universe is the effect of a system of vibration; the Cosmos is organized by the action of energy vibrating in accordance with certain rates which express themselves in form. The Universe could, therefore, in no case be anywise different than it is unless the vibratory influence that organized it had been different, the universe being the expression in form of those vibratory influences that have organized it out of the Cosmic energy or ether.

Sir William Crooks took some very fine sand and scattered it over the head of a drum. Then by taking a tuning fork and sounding different notes just above the drum head so that the vibration set in motion by this particular key would vibrate upon the drum head, the sand was seen to shift and assume a definite geometrical figure corresponding to the particular note that was produced.

When another note was sounded, the sand shifted and assumed another figure, demonstrating that the notes of a musical scale will produce a corresponding form in any substance sufficiently plastic to assume form under their direction.

This proves that vibration is the origin of form, each particular vibration giving rise to a corresponding form.

Vibration, then, is at the foundation of physics. Form, as well as light, heat, colour, and sound, are inseparably connected with vibratory activities. Each vibration expresses itself in a form corresponding to that particular rate of vibration.

Form, then, is the organized result of energy at certain rates of vibration. Vibrations express themselves in corresponding geometrical figures and in this way build up crystals that are the expression of vibration, a number of these crystals collectively forming a body of the particular elements which is the outgrowth of that particular vibration.

Study the beautiful forms of snowflakes falling on cold winter days; you will find that one day the forms are quite different from those of the day before or the day after, although the conditions may differ but in the very smallest degree.

Nevertheless, this minute difference has sufficed to evolve these very different forms, each of which is the exact expression of a special complex relation between moisture, motion, pressure, temperature, rarity, electrical tension, and chemical composition of the air that prevailed during their formation.

When a thread is introduced into a bowl of saline solution and then lifted out of it, there will gather over the entire length of the submerged string a mass of mathematically perfect crystals of salt.

It has been observed by the students of nature that the crystals are never exactly alike. Not only is this true of the different chemical elements, but we know that each individual crystal is a little different. Now, knowing that this crystallization is due to vibration and all differences in the form of the crystal are, therefore, due to differences in the rate of vibration, we can recognize the fact that the individuality of any object is due to the corresponding individuality in the vibration that gave expression to it.

It is the law of vibration that brings to maturity the fruit of every thought, whether wholesome or unwholesome, desirable or undesirable. It is this law that causes the things which we see to take form. It is this law that gives sparkle to the diamond, luster to the amethyst, colour to the grape, fragrance to the rose, beauty to the lily, and it is through the operation of this law that each of us is attracting to ourselves the associates, experiences, circumstances, conditions, and environment by which we are related to the objects and purposes which we seek.

Existence is like the output of a loom. The pattern, the design is there; but whereas our looms are mere machines, once the guiding cords have been fed into them, the loom of time is complicated by a multitude of free agents who can modify the web, making the product more beautiful or more ugly according as they are in harmony or disharmony with the general scheme.

With the Arabic numerals—1, 2, 3, 4, 5, 6, 7, 8, 9, 0—any conceivable number may be expressed.

With the twenty-six letters of the alphabet, any conceivable thought may be expressed.

With the fourteen primary elements, any conceivable thing may be organized.

What is true in the inorganic world is likewise true in the organic. Certain conscious processes will invariably be followed by the same consequence. Clearly, then, it requires an intelligent force to direct the activities of these electrons and cause them to unite with regular mathematical precision, and thus bring into being matter of every conceivable form.

Mind is then the source of all things, in the sense that the activity of mind is the initial cause of all things coming into being. This is because the primal source of all things is a corresponding thought in the Universal Mind. It is the essence of a thing that constitutes its being and the activity of mind is the cause by which the essence takes form.

An idea is a thought conceived in the mind and this rational form of the thought is the root of form in the sense that this form of thought is the initial formal expression which, acting upon substance, causes it to assume form.

There can be nothing except as there is an idea, or ideal form, engendered in the Mind. Such ideas, acting upon the Universal, engender corresponding forms.

Matter being Cosmic Mind in physical manifestation, we perceive that everything is possessed of intelligence directing its development and manifestation. This is the intelligence that causes rocks to cohere and crystallize while plants manifest life in an entirely different manner.

Plant life divides its cells rapidly, absorbs moisture, air, and light readily, while the rock expels them. But they both combine and transform elements in just the right proportions to reproduce, perpetuate, and colour their species.

The one purpose in life for centuries was as simple as that of the lower animals or plants: the simple aim of self-preservation and of the production of descendants. Human beings were contented with the simplest organic function, nutrition, and reproduction. Hunger and love were their only motives for action. For a long period, they must have aimed at the one single object at self-preservation.

In the route of our ancestry, specific lines were traveled and specific character established. We lose neither the one nor the other, for both lines and character are projected from generation to generation. The lines, although invisible, are never broken, nor are they ever abruptly changed to other type expressions. Neither are the characteristics ever lost though they continue to project from generation to generation down through the ages.

We may distill, analyze, and compound all the elements that are used as conveyors or vehicles in the process of constructive energy and we will not find the element that will produce a nut, a plum, or even as much as a mustard seed, unless we send the energy into condensation over character lines as constructive moulds that must first be established.

Character lines are invisible tracks over which and through which Nature is ever pressing into constructivity every element and thing of creation, from the plane of the fungi to that of the intellectual and spiritual man.

In its highest form of expression, the Principle of Attraction is manifested in love. It is the One Universal Principle that equally governs the seeming involuntary affinities of minerals and vegetable substances, the passion of animals, and the love of men.

The Law of Love is a piece of pure science; and the oldest and simplest form of Love is the elective affinity of two differing cells. Above all laws is the Law of Love, for Love is life.

Progress being the object of Nature, and Altruism the object of Progress, the Book of Life is found to be a love story.

A Book About You

Section Fifteen

The Imagination

You imagine many things that are not so, but if you continue to imagine these things, they eventually come to pass; why is this?

It is because the imagination is the process of imaging these things in or on your mind, and this process is nature's method of creation.

Perhaps you may think that your imagination can create nothing. Well, you can easily prove whether this is so or not yourself. Take a piece of white paper about twenty-four inches square. Draw a circle as large as this paper will permit and then draw a horizontal line through the center of the circle. Call the left end of the line 'A' and the right end 'B'. Now, draw a vertical line through the circle and call the north end of this line 'C' and the south end 'D'. Take a lead pencil and attach a string about eight inches long and upon the end of the string tie a small weight about the size of a quarter. Now, then, for the proof.

Place the paper on a table, stand upright, and hold the rod above the paper so that the pendulum will be just above the center of the paper where the lines intersect. Now think of the line A-B, but do not move; in a few minutes the pendulum will swing back and forth along the line A-B. Now think of the line C-D; the pendulum will stop swinging back and forth and will begin to swing up and down along the line C-D.

Now take your thought off from the lines entirely and fix it upon the circle. The pendulum will begin a circular motion.

Now then, think that the pendulum is swinging faster and faster, that you can hardly stop it. The motion will become so fast, that you can hardly see it go.

Now then, think that it will not move at all, that something is the matter with it.

It will stop!

This experiment is one that Mr. Charles Baudouin of The Jean Jacques Institute in France uses to illustrate the power of thought to his students.

You may think that this is will power. It is nothing of the kind. In fact, if you will the pendulum to move, it will not budge; you must think of the result, not upon how it is accomplished.

In his experiments, M. Baudouin found that the higher the type of intelligence that the student possessed the more rapidly did he secure results. Those students who were more or less deficient in mentality were very slow and in some cases results were almost negligible.

When you become familiar with the operation of this law, you will have found the secret of success, of health, of prosperity, of happiness, and of popularity.

You will have discovered a law that is as dependable as the law of gravitation.

When this law is put into operation for the purpose of bringing about material success or prosperity, it is called the Creative Law of Prosperity.

You may ask, how can this result be accomplished? How will the things be brought to you that will make you harmonious, prosperous, and happy? They will come to you through the operation of Natural Laws.

Spirit, Universal Mind, life, energy—they express through all forms of the seen and unseen side of life. The human brain is the finest, most vibrant vehicle on this plane and thus it has power or control over all things.

If you think of concentrate along any particular line, you start a train of causation; and if your thought is sufficiently concentrated and kept continuously in mind, what happens?

There is only one thing that can occur. Whatever the vision you have, the imagination you have, the image is accepted by the Universal Intelligence expressing through the cells of your physical body and environment, and these cells send out their calls into the great formless energy everywhere around you for the material that corresponds with the image and harmonizes in its vibration with it, and whether the image is for success along any particular line or fear of a particular thing, you call the atoms from out of the formless energy which make for the success or the thing you fear—you relate with conditions necessary to bring into manifestation the thing you desire or the thing you fear.

Thoughts of anger, hatred, fear, jealousy, worry, etc. act directly on the secretions causing an actual poison in the system, which in time will destroy the body unless they are overcome with love, harmony, joy, faith, etc. Constructive thoughts and love is the strongest of all.

We are told by the greatest of teachers that the fundamental or foundation law of our being is love. Love God, love your neighbour, love yourself, love your enemy, love everybody and everything. No one can afford to hate because hate always destroys the hater. It is said that "Whom the gods would destroy, they first make angry."

Prosperity is a harmonious, creative state of being. Creative law will overcome every kind of inharmony, whether it be financial, physical, mental, moral, or social.

Every thought of lack or poverty acts directly on the heart, affecting the circulation causing constipation, congestion, and many forms of disease due to poor circulation.

Thoughts of prosperity, love, joy, and happiness also act upon the heart, causing good circulation and a healthy body. There is much truth in the sayings "Laugh and grow fat" and "A merry heart doeth good like a medicine."

Any physician will tell you that if he can get a good circulation of pure blood to the part or organ of the body affected, he can heal it, regardless as to what may appear to be the difficulty.

All possession is based on consciousness. All gain is the result of an accumulative consciousness. All loss is the result of a scattering consciousness. This is another way of saying that thoughts are things and that things are thoughts—what one thinks materializes. Thoughts are today being photographed showing that they take form in the surrounding ether, or universal substance. These are scientific facts.

Thought is a creative energy and will automatically correlate with it object and bring it into manifestation because thought is spiritual energy or vibration.

All this brings us back to the fact that prosperity is the result of right, or creative, thinking and that poverty is the result of wrong, or destructive, thinking.

You can prove this for yourself in a very short time.

Begin by taking these words: "I am whole, perfect, strong, powerful, loving, harmonious, prosperous, and happy." Repeat them over and over to yourself as often as you can think to do it, especially the last thing before dropping off to sleep at night and the first thing upon awaking in the morning. Remember, these are creative words.

Every thought or word opposed to them is destructive and must not be allowed to enter your mind or to be expressed in words. Every thought of disease, sickness, and pain is opposed to wholeness and perfection and should be eliminated by declaring, "I am whole and perfect!" Every thought of weakness is opposed to strength and should be put out of mind by saying, "I am strong and powerful!"

To know this law and live in harmony with it is to build prosperity on a rock foundation which nothing can destroy.

By this law, things which are seen are made from things which do not appear.

We are told by scientific students of nature that every element in the material world is in the ether. From these elements, the cabbage takes what it requires to form a cabbage. From these same elements, the apple tree forms and colours an apple, and the rose from these elements produces, colours, and perfumes a rose. Surely, man should know as much as the cabbage, the apple, or the rose about handling these elements.

Students of nature also tell us that there is one universal substance out of which all things are formed and that the difference between flesh, vegetable, stone, iron, glass, etc. is the difference in the vibration, or motion, of these particles of substance as they are brought together and act and react upon each other.

If you send thoughts of health, love, and prosperity, they will return to you multiplied like the seed you sow in your garden. Send out destructive thoughts, they also return to you multiplied like weeds. You reap what you sow.

Law governs every form of light, heat, sound, and energy. Law governs every material thing and every immaterial thought. Law covers the earth with beauty and fills it with bounty. Shall you then not be certain that it also governs the distribution of this bounty?

There are, however, many laws with which, possibly, you may not be familiar. For instance, when you grow weary of listening to a piece of jazz music being broadcasted form a New York hotel, you turn the dial an eighth of an inch and you get the beautiful notes of a violin from Detroit or Cleveland or Chicago. Again, you turn the dial an eighth of an inch and you hear an organ solo from Omaha or Denver. Another turn of the dial and you hear a quartette singing in San Francisco or Los Angeles. And this is true whether you live in an apartment in New York or a bungalow on the Hawaiian Islands or are the keeper of a lighthouse on the shores of Alaska.

The simple turn of a dial will take you clear across the continent and you may stop as often as you wish on the way, and all because the various broadcasting stations use a different wave length.

The wave length depends upon the frequency or the number of vibrations that pass a given point in one second.

It is possible for one of the more powerful broadcasting stations to send a message which will simultaneously reach every person in the United States, but the message will be received by those only who have a receiver that is in tune with the station which is sending the message.

The seven planets comprising the Solar System are all creating vibrations in the ether. These vibrations are all of such high frequency that there is at this time no means of measuring them.

These vibrations change the character of the thought, the emotions, the impulses, and thus influence the lives of every vital organism.

And why should this not be true? The message from an ordinary broadcasting station is delivered with energy equal to something like 5,000 HP while a planet like Jupiter with a diameter of 85,000 miles develops an almost inconceivable amount of energy as it plows its way through the ether with the speed of a cannon ball.

It is Nature's method in comparison with the methods of man, but you are inclined to magnify the results of man's endeavours and minimize or deny the influence of the greatest amount of physical force in existence.

When you repeat, "I am prosperous, harmonious, and happy," you are tuning in on Jupiter, the most powerful station in existence.

You are raising your vibration, you are increasing the frequency, you are shortening the wavelength.

Jupiter is the station of good fortune, the station of power, the station of plenty.

Get him located on your mental dial.

PETER BELL

He moved among the vales and streams,
In the green wood and hollow dell;
    They were his dwelling night and day
    But Nature ne'er could find the way
Into the heart of Peter Bell.

In vain through every changing year,
Did Nature lead him as before,
    A primrose by the river's brim,
    A yellow primrose was to him,
And it was nothing more.

                    –Wordsworth

A Book About You

Section Sixteen

Destiny

Beauty always accompanies economy of structure and movement, indeed it is the expression of this economy. All improvement in speed and directness of movement must have been adaptive, must have given the individual an advantage in gaining food, escaping enemies, or in some way making its evolutionary position more secure.

Beauty and intelligence are the outcome of different phases of the same forces of organic evolution. What is good we call beautiful.

A graceful carriage, a springing, vigorous, rhythmical step, a sweet breath, good teeth, clear complexion, a pleasant musical voice, a handsome shapely neck, red lips, a well-developed chin, and clear, bright, animated eyes are indications of health.

The ideals of human excellence, of character, morality, beauty, intelligence, health, sanity, and energy that we teach our young men and women cause them to seek these things in their mates.

The ideals are thus bred into the physical and mental constitution of the race. They become its most priceless possession.

And because this stream of germ plasm is almost inviolable, it comes about that when a race has attained to health and character by means of natural selection, these virtues can be bequeathed to succeeding generations until the river of life empties into the ocean of eternity.

In order to maintain the equality of the sees in numbers and quality, nature has ordained that in each succeeding generation, the elements of human character shall cross the line of genesis.

The history of the world reveals that fact that men do not transmit their characteristics to their sons. Neither do women transmit their characteristics to their daughters.

No great man has ever yet appeared who did not have a mother who embodied in her character the elements which made him successful. No woman has ever astonished the world with her genius who was not the offspring of a father who possessed the germs of the same genius.

Differences in environment and education have had their influence, but as far as the law of inheritance furnishes a cause of observed effects, there are no exceptions to this rule.

In any apparent exception where a son has followed in the footsteps of his father with success, it will be found that the mother possessed the elements of character that made the success possible.

In all ages, men have mourned the fact that their sons were unable to follow in their footsteps, while the current theology and social customs of society have denied this success to their daughters, because the occupation in which those talents would shine have not been considered within "woman's sphere."

And so, after decades of misuse and suppression, the talent has appeared in the grandson. In the same way, talented boys inheriting from sensitive and refined mothers the grace which would have made them brilliant musicians, accomplished painters, and incomparable poets have been compelled to adopt commercial pursuits for which they were utterly unfitted.

Good examples of this transference of acquired development to the opposite sex in the third generation are found in the pedigrees of trotting horses. The highly trained stallion George Wilkes does not appear as the sire of any of the very fast mares, but he appears ten times as the sire's sire and as many more times as the sire's grandsire.

Martin Kallikak believed that blood would not tell; or, if it did tell, it would not tell on him. Martin's dramatic history and the history of his germ cells, his blood, have been related in a little book called "The Kallikak Family"[1] by Dr. Henry H. Goddard, Director of the Juvenile

---

[1] *The Kallikak Family: A Study in the Heredity of Feeble-Mindedness* was first published in 1912. "Kallikak" is a pseudonym from the Greek words "kalos" and "kakos", which mean "good" and "bad" respectively.

Research Bureau of the State of Ohio and formerly Superintendent of the famous School of Feeble-Minded at Vineland, New Jersey.

Martin Kallikak was a young soldier of the Revolutionary War. His ancestry was excellent. But one wild night up the Hudson River, Martin forgot his noble blood. In this night of dissipation, he met a physically attractive, feeble-minded girl. The result of that meeting was a feeble-minded boy. This boy grew up and married a woman of whose mentality Doctor Goddard could secure no record. But she was evidently of the same ilk. They produced numerous progeny with a large percentage of feeble-mindedness. These grew up lazy, thrift-less, shiftless, trifling, thieving people. Marrying into their own kind, another generation of the same general character came upon the human scene. This has gone on now for six generations.

However, on the other side of the canvas, blood has painted a different and wonderful story. Later in his life, Martin married a young Quaker woman of splendid talents and heroic ancestry. It seemed that this line of children simply could not turn out badly in any environment. Indeed, like all blood, good or bad, it made its own environment. This line has given us 496 descendants. All have been normal people. As Doctor Goddard says, they have given us descendants of the highest respectability and social usefulness including among their members "doctors, lawyers, judges, educators, landholders, traders, and men and women prominent in every phase of social life." The last one on the chart is now a man of wealth and influence.

Nobody ever had to build asylums, penitentiaries, reformatories, or special schools for this line of blood. The other line has cost society hundreds of thousands of dollars to restrain their evil tendencies and care for their feeble minds and bodies. One line has torn down, the other has built up; one line has reaped, and the other has scattered; one has contributed nothing but wickedness and woe, while the other has blessed the earth with beauty and achievement.

Thus we find the difference in individual lives to be largely measured by the degree of intelligence which they manifest. It is a greater intelligence that placed the animal in a higher scale of being than the plant, the man higher than the animal; and we find this increased intelligence is again indicted by the power of the individual to control modes of action and thus to consciously adjust himself to his environment.

It is this adjustment that occupies the attention of the greatest minds and this adjustment consists in the recognition of an existing order in the Universal Mind, for it is well known that this mind will obey us precisely in proportion as we first obey it.

As we increase in experience and development, there is a corresponding increase in the exercise of the intellect—in the range and power of feeling, in the ability to choose, in the power of will, in all executive action, in all self-consciousness.

The success of the hour may belong to the strongest fighter, but the future belongs to him who knows best how to adapt himself to the most precarious condition of life.

The gigantic animals that lived at remote geological periods have vanished, but many of their weaker contemporaries still exist.

Choose what improvements you wish in a flower, a fruit, or a tree and by crossing, selection, cultivation, and persistence it can be fixed irrevocably.

Choose any trait of character, be it honesty, fairness, purity, industry, or thrift, by giving all that is implied in healthful, environmental influence, you can cultivate it and fix it there for life.

Heredity will, of course, make itself felt, and as in the plant under improvement, there will be certain strong tendencies to reversion, but persistence will win.

If you are highly ambitious and are devouring biographies of this great genius or that powerful captain of industry for cues to success, it will be well to take an inventory of the endowments given the great genius during the formative period of his life.

Cosmic Intelligence continues to experiment and develops other coordinated systems into higher and higher complex organizations.

Experiment after experiment is tried and different specie organizations developed, each one trying to keep the spark of life burning within itself to its highest degree by continually adjusting itself to the changed conditions of its environment.

The protoplasm or cell perceives its environment, initiates motion, and chooses its food. These are evidences of mind. As an organism develops and becomes more complex, the cells begin to specialize, some doing one thing and some doing another, but all of them showing intelligence. By association, their mind powers increase.

Whereas in the beginning each function of life and each action is the result of conscious thought, the habitual actions become automatic or subconscious in order that the self-conscious mind may attend to other things. The new actions will, however, in their turn become habitual, then automatic, then subconscious in order that the mind again may be free from this detail and advance to still other activities.

Human love has as many elements and shades as there are phases of human consciousness and interest. It includes emotional enthusiasm, tenderness, and devotion; aesthetic attractiveness, appreciation, and satisfaction; intellectual stimulation, approval, and respect; social acquaintance, companionship, and comradeship, and the happiness which is the result of self-denying consideration and sacrificing service.

This means that self-consciousness is increasing, expanding, growing, developing, and enlarging. It increases and develops because it is a spiritual activity. We multiply our possession of spiritual things in proportion to our use of them. All material things are consumed in the using. There is a diametrically opposite law governing the use of the spiritual and the material.

The intellectuals are not necessarily the great benefactors of mankind because as a rule their noble ideas have not the emotion to propel them to success. You undoubtedly know many who have been too dumb to recognize opposition and so accomplished what our intellectuals said "could not be done."

Combine proper, intelligent, well-born emotion with an idea and it is like combining energy to mass—it goes forth with direction and force to bless the world with its goods. Deny the idea, however nobly conceived, this mysterious quality and it is likely to die at birth.

You are made up of millions of minute living creatures each possessing mind and intelligence. These are controlled by group minds, and these group minds are controlled by the subconscious mind, which in turn is controlled by the thought which enters it.

It is thought which makes the adjustment.

This is the process of crossing the human with the germ of the Divine.

This is the infusion of a higher type.

This is the final goal of human destiny!

THE END

Index

A

Adams, Professor 42, 43
adrenal 127, 128
Air 6, 73
Airy 72
Alpha Centauri 65
Aquarius 26, 51, 61, 67, 68, 72, 120
Aries 11, 51, 52, 53, 67, 68, 72, 81
aspect 8, 14, 29, 38, 49, 50, 96
astral essences 13
Auriga 54
Autumn Quarter 119

B

Baha, Abdul 15
Baudouin, Charles 156
Boker 97
Bradley, Burton 90
Burbank, Luther 29
Byron, George Gordon 105

C

Callizo, Jean 77
Cambridge Observatory 42
Cancer 11, 26, 51, 55, 67, 68, 72
Capricorn 11, 26, 51, 60, 67, 68, 72
cardiac 13
cardinal plexus 140
cardinal sign 55, 68
Castor 53
cavernous 13
cerebrospinal system 137
Collier, Nate 134
Copper 21
Cosmic-consciousness 30, 31
Creative Law of Prosperity 156
Crooks, Sir William 149

D

dendrites 25
Divine Creation 8

dreams 25

E

Earth 1, 2, 6, 9, 10, 11, 20, 21, 25, 26,
    37, 38, 39, 40, 41, 44, 46, 48,
    49, 66, 67, 72, 76, 77, 78, 79,
    117, 123, 124
Earthy 71, 72, 124
ecliptic 21
Edison 4, 126
electro-magnetic 3
electron 5, 35, 79
emotions 22, 38, 39, 53, 55, 62, 63,
    71, 72, 73, 82, 88, 89, 93, 95,
    116, 119, 135, 136, 139, 145,
    160
energy 1, 3, 4, 9, 11, 12, 15, 17, 18,
    20, 25, 26, 36, 40, 44, 45, 67,
    69, 75, 76, 77, 78, 79, 80, 81,
    86, 87, 90, 92, 93, 94, 97, 99,
    100, 101, 102, 103, 104, 105,
    106, 107, 108, 109, 111, 112,
    116, 117, 123, 125, 128, 129,
    135, 136, 137, 138, 139, 140,
    141, 142, 144, 149, 150, 152,
    156, 157, 158, 159, 160, 163,
    168
Epicurus 24
epigastric 13
ether 1, 2, 3, 5, 6, 10, 12, 22, 25, 30,
    32, 44, 76, 78, 79, 80, 81, 86,
    87, 88, 89, 92, 95, 101, 111,
    116, 125, 149, 158, 160

F

Faraday, Michael 35
Faraday Effect 35
fear 8, 15, 32, 50, 89, 95, 110, 117,
    139, 140, 144, 157
Fiery 72
Fire 6, 73
fixed sign 68
free will 7

G

Gallac, Dr. 43
Gemini 26, 51, 53, 54, 67, 68, 72
glands 32, 127, 128, 129, 130, 135
Goddard, Dr. Henry H. 164, 165
Gold 21
gravitation 102, 103, 156
Greeks 65

H

helium 102
Herschel, Sir John 42
Hyades 54

I

Illuminati 127
inertia 46, 118
infrared 92
Ingersoll, Robert G. 121
Iron 21, 90
Isaiah 133
Isis 9

J

Jupiter 9, 10, 12, 13, 14, 17, 19, 21, 22, 23, 24, 40, 41, 43, 44, 45, 46, 49, 117, 160

K

Kallikak, Martin 164, 165
kinetic 1, 80, 81, 101

L

laryngeal 13
Law of Attraction 125, 144
Law of Causation 125
Law of Love 144, 153
law of periodicity 115, 116
Law of Sevens 115
Law of Universal Gravitation 103
Lead 21
Leo 26, 51, 55, 56, 67, 68, 72, 119

Le Verrier 43
Libra 11, 26, 51, 57, 67, 68, 72
Lodge, Sir Joseph Oliver 35
Loeb, Prof. Jaques 126
Longfellow, Henry Wadsworth 3, 83
Lowell, James Russell 63
Lycurgus 127

M

magnetism 8, 13, 14, 36, 56, 102, 103, 105, 115, 143, 144
Markham, Edwin 108
Mars 9, 10, 12, 13, 15, 17, 19, 21, 22, 23, 39, 40, 43, 44, 45, 46, 52, 81
Mercury 9, 10, 12, 13, 17, 19, 21, 22, 23, 31, 37, 38, 44, 45, 46, 110
Messenger of the Gods 37
Monroe, Dr. 132
Moon 9, 11, 12, 13, 19, 21, 22, 25, 26, 36, 37, 67, 68, 124
mutable sign 56, 59, 68

N

Neptune 9, 10, 12, 17, 23, 37, 43, 44, 47
neurons 25
Newton, Isaac 103
noise 85

O

Oneness, theory of 138
Orion 54
Osler, Sir William 127

P

pancreas 127, 128, 129
Paracelsus 127
parallax 66
pendulum 155, 156
personal consciousness 28
pharyngeal 13
pineal 127, 128

Pisces 26, 51, 54, 62, 67, 68, 72
pituitary 127, 129
plexi 13, 129
Pollux 53
potential 1, 80, 81, 87, 101, 116, 131
pranic energy 111
Principle of Attraction 145, 153
prostatic 13
Ptolemy 65
Pythagorus 127

Q

Quicksilver 21

R

radio waves 75
reflex 78, 106
Revelations 17
rhythmical breathing 111, 112

S

sacral 13
sacrum plexus 140
Sagittarius 26, 51, 59, 67, 68, 72
Saturn 9, 10, 12, 13, 14, 15, 17, 18,
      19, 21, 22, 23, 41, 43, 44, 45,
      46, 47, 49, 50, 61, 117, 118
Scorpio 26, 51, 58, 67, 68, 72, 119
secretions 32, 127, 128, 129, 157
Self-consciousness 30
self-determination 7
sensory stimuli 25
Septimal Law 115
Seven Norms 13
sex glands 127, 129
Silence, the 33
Silver 21
Simple Consciousness 30
solar fluid 80
solar plexus 135, 137, 140, 143
Solar Science 47
spleen 9, 117, 140
Spring Quarter 118
Stephenson, George 104

Summer Quarter 119
Sun 19, 21, 22, 23, 25, 26, 36, 37,
      38, 39, 41, 42, 43, 50, 52, 55,
      56, 57, 58, 59, 60, 61, 62, 66,
      67, 68, 73, 77, 78, 86, 87, 100,
      104, 114, 116, 117, 123, 124,
      129
sympathetic nervous system 13, 32,
      111, 117, 136, 138, 140, 143,
      144, 145

T

Taurus 26, 51, 52, 53, 67, 68, 72
thymus 127, 128
thyroid 127, 128, 129
Tin 21

U

ultrared rays 130
ultraviolet rays 129, 130
Universal Mind 15, 31, 125, 151, 156,
      166
Uranus 9, 10, 12, 17, 23, 42, 43, 44,
      47, 67, 81, 118

V

Valentin 127
Venus 9, 10, 12, 13, 14, 15, 17, 19,
      21, 22, 23, 24, 38, 39, 44, 45
vibratory activity 1, 2, 3, 4, 6, 91, 93,
      102
Virgo 26, 51, 56, 57, 67, 68, 72

W

Wagner 127
war 12, 81, 82, 121, 165
Water 6, 72, 105, 126
Watery 71, 72
Winter Quarter 119

Z

Zodiac 8, 11, 12, 13, 14, 20, 43, 44,
      50, 52, 53, 55, 56, 57, 58, 59,
      60, 61, 62, 67, 80, 118

Biography of Charles F. Haanel

Charles F. Haanel was born in Ann Arbor, Michigan on May 22, 1866. He received many degrees, including hon. Ph.D., College National Electronic Institute; Metaphysics, Psy. D., College of Divine Metaphysics; and M.D., Universal College of Dupleix, India. He is the ex-President of the Continental Commercial Company and the ex-President of the Sacramento Valley Improvement Company.

He is the author of works on philosophy, psychology, causation, science of living, personality, and science of mind, synthesized in *The Master Key System*, a system of philosophy for application to the affairs of everyday life.

Mr. Haanel was affiliated with many groups, including Fellow London College of Psychotherapy; member Authors' League of America; American Society of Psychical Research; member of the Society of Rosicrucians; the American Suggestive Therapeutical Association; Science League of America; Pi Gamma Mu Fraternity; Master Mason, Keystone Lodge No. 243, A.F. & A.M.; created a Noble in Moolah Temple.

Mr. Haanel died on November 27, 1949 at the age of 83. He was buried in Bellefontaine Cemetery, St. Louis.

For more information, visit **www.haanel.com**.

KALLISTI

The Master Key System
Charles F. Haanel

Master Key Arcana
Charles F. Haanel
& others

**The Amazing Secrets o
the Yogi**
Charles F. Haanel

**The Master Key
Workbook**
Tony Michalski
& Robert Schmitz

A Book About You
Charles F. Haanel

The New Psychology
Charles F. Haanel

Walk, Don't Run
Steven "Rusty" Johnson

**Getting Connected
Through Exceptional
Leadership**
Karl Walinskas

Mental Chemistry
Charles F. Haanel